THE TROUBLE WITH LOVING POETS AND OTHER ESSAYS ON FAILURE

THE TROUBLE WITH LOVING POETS AND OTHER ESSAYS ON FAILURE

ELIZABETH ZALESKI

Belt Publishing

First Edition 2026
ISBN: 9781540270146

Belt Publishing

www.beltpublishing.com

Cover design by David Wilson
Book design by Julie Foster

Audiobook: The galaxy is a place of laws.
Me (mishearing): *Yes, yes, of loss.*

TABLE OF (DIS)CONTENTS

WITH FAMILY

VEGETABLE PSYCHOLOGY, LOVESICK ASTROLOGY

The first time I saw my dad without his hair was in a crowded restaurant, where the overhead lights emphasized all the subtle dents and ridges he'd revealed. Two days earlier, he had shaved his head. All that thick, brown, respectable hair—gone. Now he was sitting across from my brother and me, studying the menu and trying to buy psychedelics. He leaned forward but didn't lower his voice: "Do you think you could get me some mushrooms?"

Though unexpected, this request was in some ways less surprising than if Dad had decided to order fried mushrooms for an appetizer, as he hadn't eaten anything resembling a vegetable since 1997, when I was thirteen years old. That was the last time he'd tried eating lettuce and the first time I heard him say "fuck," as in, "I try to eat lettuce, but I just fucking *hate* it." Still, the question was out of character for my dad, who could barely drink alcohol and had never smoked marijuana.

My brother was in his second year of college, and I had graduated from that same college a few months earlier. Mom and Dad had called each of us the night before and told us they were coming down to Columbus "just to visit." My parents had a tradition of taking us out to the most impersonal places—a Chili's, a Damon's Grill, any chain restaurant with gigantic television screens and fried mozzarella sticks—and making dire announcements midmeal (Mom: I found a lump in my breast, Dad: The dog is dead), so I was wary. A week before my sister's first wedding, Mom took my sister and me to Damon's and told us that she'd been having regular affairs with Dad's consent since we were kids. I cried into my rib basket.

My parents had driven two hours to see us, and after I decided on the chicken fingers, I sat and waited. I assumed they were there to announce that they were finally splitting up. Their marriage had been floundering for years, and Dad's sudden interest in mushrooms had me picturing him in the deep end, down a few feet in the greenish murk, kicking. I figured tripping with Mom was either a desperate plan to reconnect or a desperate last hurrah.

Maybe, I considered, they'd finally exhausted all the legal possibilities for making each other interesting. Because my parents are honest, funny, and candid, but also because they have never fully understood that your children are not your friends, I know rather too much about those possibilities. During my late teens, if I needed to retrieve something from the basement while friends were over, I had to invent reasons why they couldn't accompany me—otherwise, I'd have to explain the giant sex swing crouched in the corner like an eight-foot-tall spider with four legs.

"Rats," I would venture. "Sewage backup."

Mom had laughingly told me not long before the night at the restaurant that she now used it as a regular swing, sans sex. This same commitment to transparency now placed my father in front of us, asking his son to buy him illegal drugs.

"Come on, it'll be fun," Dad said now, pressuring my brother like the bad kid in black jeans in an after-school special.

"No," my brother said, like Nancy Reagan.

Because my brother was the youngest in the family, he had been spared the trip to Damon's the week before my sister's first wedding

Dad jabbed a french fry at his plate a few times while he considered his final words on the subject. “I don’t know. But I’m getting old,” he said. “I need to see some new things.”

• • • • • • •

A few days later, I decided to drive up to my parents’ house and spend the weekend. I figured by Sunday, either Mom or Dad would tell me why they were acting so weirdly. Now it was Sunday, and it was dreary and rainy outside. The muddy creek at the bottom of the sloped front yard crept ever closer to the fence along the border. Valentine’s Day was Wednesday, and Mom was making Reuben sandwiches. She wrapped them in tinfoil and talked, downright bright-eyed, about what makes a classic Reuben. “Corned beef, sauerkraut, Swiss cheese, and Thousand Island dressing.” She said the Thousand Island dressing was the secret, but she was fretting over not having rye bread.

I watched her as she clucked her tongue and muttered, “I just wish I had some rye bread. It’s really not complete without the rye.”

Mom hadn’t made a hot sandwich since I was a kid, and the subtly layered creations eating up the counter space in front of me were not sloppy joes or Steak-umms. I thought about how unhappy she’d been in our company at dinner last week and how Dad was losing all that weight. I thought, “She’s awful intent on that rye bread.” Then, “She’s having an affair.”

It wasn’t a shock. In fact, a part of me was relieved to know that the trouble I sensed was just an affair and not something more serious, like one of them carrying around a giant abdominal tumor. The other part was angry with Mom. In those days, I usually sided with Dad in their fights—not because there was anything like a clear right or wrong in the bizarre world of my parents' half-open marriage (my father has been monogamous his whole life) but because Mom's actions had consequences that affected me directly, led to confusing handshakes with men I'd never met before and would never see again. Meanwhile, Dad's voyeurism and encouragement remained hidden behind bedroom doors and in parts of my brain I'd draped curtains over.

I wanted to have a conversation, to be clean and quick, and avoid the sniffling, aching mess this situation sometimes led to.

"Who are you cooking those sandwiches for?"

"A friend at work."

"Are you having an affair?"

"No," she said. She held the word for emphasis, making it clear that she wasn't surprised I'd asked.

I was fairly sure she was lying. After the dinner at Damon's and some therapy, I'd suggested to my parents that perhaps it would be healthier for us all if we imposed some boundaries on the type of information they shared with us kids. It was possible, I suggested, that knowing Mom could easily reach orgasm in any of the most popular sexual positions was not vital to my feeling close to her. None of us ever took this advice seriously, including me, but as a result of my having introduced the idea, Mom sometimes lied about her relationships with men other than my father, as if she'd suddenly, if only occasionally, adopted the position that I might be too delicate to know such things.

I thought back over the last few months and piled up evidence. There was the time over the summer I had gone to get something out of her car at work and was surprised by a bottle of lube in the console. This was incriminating, as most of Mom's affairs started at work, but not conclusive. Then there was her curious reaction over the Thanksgiving dinner she tried to save, also for "a friend at work," which was prematurely devoured by the dog—she grew teary-eyed over the ravages of turkey and mashed potatoes. There were the three prior affairs to consider, and now, the six gleaming sandwiches she was wrapping, the foil making a racket.

"Can I have one?"

"Sure," she said.

I ate it and glared at her.

• • • • • • •

My dad is a very smart man who makes very stupid mistakes. One of his friends at work—a young guy working on his PhD—told him once that he'd given up on talking with the other PhDs there about his ideas. They didn't seem to have a clue, he said, while Dad followed along and gave useful advice with just his BS from nearly three decades ago. But at home with us, the sort of sound reasoning Dad's friend relied on occasionally goes missing—like the time he burned a pile of straw under a pine tree because he said green things didn't burn. Seconds after the straw ignited, the flames rode up the trunk, and the top of the tree exploded like God calling Moses. The fire was reaching for the house with red-orange hands.

My brother, who was twelve at the time, disappeared. Then he burst out the front door and ran straight to the tree, heaving a single full glass of water onto the inferno.

Dad told me later that he loved my brother for that moment, for believing he could save us all with his single cup, and no less for the slumped shoulders and disappointed exhale that followed as the flames continued to crackle. Mom screamed obscenities while I waved the cordless phone around offering to call the fire department. Dad grabbed a garden hose and doused the tree until the blaze fizzled into steam.

I'm not sure if Dad tells that story at work or if, like his basement tinkering with homemade perpetual motion machines—chimerical according to the first law of thermodynamics—he keeps it to himself in the company of fellow engineers. I've seen all manner of things crash and burn in my father's path, only to hear him explain what just went wrong with an answer straight from a physics book. Once, I dropped my cell phone from a considerable height directly into a cup of water. Dad, having heard of some trick for drying electronics out, remembered incorrectly and tried the microwave, which resulted in fireworks and a melted screen. "Oh yeeeah," he said, unabashed. "You can't put metal in microwaves." He went on to spell out the science behind the carnage in great detail. Then it occurred to him, quite joyfully: "Incubator! That's what you're supposed to use." While his mistakes are always brainless, raised Catholic, he can also summon elegant confessions.

•••••••

A few days after I asked my mom if she was having an affair, Valentine's Day came and went. No mushrooms were ingested, hallucinogenic or otherwise. Then Mom moved out of the house and in with her boyfriend. I did not know his name and did not seek it out. I found it was easier to call him "Asshole" or "Dickhead."

Meanwhile, Dad set up a telescope he had recently received for twenty-five years of service with his roller-bearing company. He read that Venus was looming large, but he couldn't find it.

In response to his phone call shortly after Mom moved out, I found myself home again, sitting across from him in the hot yellow light that reflected off the kitchen table. He sat with his palms facing up on the tabletop. He was assuring me that he wouldn't try to kill himself again and showed me a can of lentil soup to prove it.

He pointed to the yellow ribbon printed on the label. "Look, a full serving of vegetables in every bowl."

He'd tried twice over the last three days, but he told me they were half-hearted attempts. The first time, he downed a handful of sleeping pills and then immediately realized he didn't actually want to die. What he really wanted was for Mom to stumble upon his dead body and feel very, very sorry for him, so he went to the kitchen, mixed a tablespoon of salt into a cup of tap water, drank it, and threw up the pills.

Later, his emotions got all tangled up again, and he forgot the difference he'd spotted between wanting to kill himself and wanting to make Mom feel guilty, so he worked up a numerical pattern and then started all the engines in the garage. The pattern was this: ten times into the room, starting with ten breaths and increasing by ten each trip. He'd be dead far before he hit 470.

He set about his task, plodding in and out of the garage, increasingly foggy-headed in the building carbon monoxide. Before long, like a referee of corporeality, the carbon monoxide detector at the far end of the house went off, the shrill, relentless chirp calling Dad's bluff. *Danger, danger!* it called, reminding him of the tag-along body he'd almost forgotten as his mind raced outward into a vast plane of desperation and despair. The little batteries powered an angry shout, which compressed his anxiety to the immediate problem of oxygen.

He was overcome with a profound sense of guilt for the life he had almost thrown away: that of Duncan, his dog, who would have been trapped in the house while the carbon monoxide continued to build. Duncan, the clairvoyant, who months before had heroically devoured Asshole's turkey dinner. Dad threw open the windows and turned off the engines, worrying all the while that he was too late.

The first thing I told him was that I was sorry he had wanted to die. Then I told him to stop fucking around. After all, I'd gone to therapy to talk about more than just my parents' weird relationship—I'd also gone to talk about my recurring feeling of wanting to be dead. As someone familiar with fantasies of oblivion, I felt that Dad was approaching his own suicidal thinking less as a crisis than a line to toe, a line he'd twice crossed only to be yanked back by tethers I didn't trust would continue to hold. When the next lull of lonely hours descended, would a full serving of vegetables keep him alive? I told him to call me the next time he thought about destroying himself.

Mom came over a few hours later because Dad had told her I was in town and I'd stopped answering her calls. We sat in the downstairs living room and yelled at each other. I said something about being on suicide watch and got choked up.

"What?" she asked and looked at my dad.

"Yeah, I've been feeling pretty down," he said, looking at the floor.

"Are you stupid?" she shouted. "The next time you think about killing yourself, you call me. You don't call your kids about that shit!" She started to cry then too.

After some more yelling, she tried to leave, but her car got stuck in the snow at the bottom of the driveway. "Need a push," she huffed after tramping back up the slippery hill. Dad suited up and was marvelously happy to get her unstuck and back on her way to Dickhead.

Watching Dad lace up his boots and cover his shaved head with a trapper hat, I wondered how my parents would have transformed had they eaten mushrooms on Valentine's Day. Would their bodies have gained a new splendor and warmth in the oversized house? Or would panic have set in as each registered the deep-set eyes, the lined and tired skin that insulated the person across the room, and the terrible distance that grew between their inward-rushing minds?

• • • • • • •

Later that evening, I stepped out onto the second-story porch and saw Dad crouched awkwardly over his telescope. Out in the farther reaches, the stars were not merely far away but hurriedly fleeing, a fact my father grasped so palpably that he sometimes called for an ambulance. A gigantic yellow moon hung bald-faced above the pine trees, but Dad was still looking for Venus.

Metaphorically convenient, this detail is also true, just as it's true that the moon was utterly resplendent. The evening and everyone in it were aglow—stupidly, shimmeringly aglow. I was waiting for him to turn around and see it.

THE SWEEPER AND THE RESIDUE

THE SWEEPER

Under the scrutinizing eye of my mother, my childhood homes were kept very clean. Though the tools and methods we employed in the tasks of cleanliness were unexceptional, the language was not. When at least once a week, we steered a detritus-sucking machine over the carpet, we were "sweeping," not "vacuuming," and we always did so with a "sweeper," never a "vacuum." Sweeping, along with dusting and scrubbing the toilet, belonged to a set of activities we called "cleaning," but when referring to the surface-level tidying hastily performed prior to a guest's arrival or when putting things back in their rightful place, we used the rare Scots-Irish form "redd up."

There was twice as much carpet to sweep these days, as our domestic mess had begun to sprawl. Instead of living together in one house, my parents had recently divorced and now lived in two. One of these dwellings was a tiny, pink-carpeted upstairs apartment my father rented from a woman named Carol, who lived downstairs with her husband and thirteen cats, and one evening, I found myself, along with my brother, my dad, and Carol the landlord, crammed into Dad's living room for a sweeper demonstration. Carol had made it known that despite owning thirteen shedding cats, she swept but once a year. She was a tough sell, you might say, for my mom, who was there to wow us with her high-quality, American-made, air-purifying sweeper.

Mom had recently bought her own house and then promptly lost her factory job. She needed three sales before the sweeper company would put her on the payroll. I hadn't seen Mom in some time, partly because I lived two hours away and partly because the particulars of the divorce meant we were often mad at each other, and I noticed she was wearing a strappy turquoise top and black pants, neither of which I'd ever seen before. Her cheeks were flushed and she looked flustered. I was struck, as I often am, by how beautiful she is—high cheekbones, auburn hair, a perfectly proportioned body. Moments before, she had dumped baking soda onto the rosy carpet and mashed it into the fibers with her thin, ringless fingers—it was funny, what with the landlord there and all. Next, she took Dad's sweeper, a cheap little aqua-blue Eureka, and ran it over the powdery spot until we, playing the part of the dubious crowd, were satisfied that she'd given the Boss-Pro a fair run at the dust.

Then Mom consulted her notes briefly, strapped a suitable hose extension onto her product, and fiddled with the power switches a moment. Suddenly the Filterqueen Majestic was roaring away over that same square of carpet, which to the naked eye looked clear of baking soda. She called our attention to the particles of white powder leaping about in a small, squat, see-through cylinder attached midway up the length of the hose—we could see the leavings of the Eureka dancing inside like flakes in a dirty snow globe. After a minute, she quieted the sweeper and removed a filter from the viewing cylinder. She looked triumphant as she dramatically plopped the white disc onto the floor, its cache of baking soda erupting right back onto the carpet.

Eureka. She'd proved it: no marks on the surface, you see, but deep down there, nestled in the pink fibers of our lives, was a dirty residue. This wasn't a mess we could simply redd up—no, we'd have to buy a new sweeper and clean.

THE RESIDUE

After she lost her job at the factory and before she started selling sweepers, my mom had tried driving a semitruck. It was summer, and she optimistically enrolled in a class with her boyfriend, Doug, a man I knew simply as a ne'er-do-well with a litter of kids and warrants in his wake. She paid to fix his meth-rotted teeth, paid off his fines, and paid his and her tuition. He punched her in the face the night after their first class, though if you asked her, she'd say, unironically, "He's never punched me in the face, only strangled me." The people in the adjoining hotel room called the cops, and when they arrived, Mom and the boyfriend were asked to leave. She declined pressing charges.

The truck-driving school was in Columbus, where I lived, so Mom had visited me after the incident and indignantly stomped around my apartment, fresh bruises streaked like mud across her cheek and neck. Then she went back to her new house and threw all of Doug's belongings into her yard.

Later on in the summer, she returned to the school alone, and for a few days, she and I found ourselves sharing my brother's room in the dank basement of the empty college house he and his housemates rented during the school year. Mom and I mopped up after the leaky toilet in the laundry room and made an odd pair of students ourselves. She stretched on the couch in the afternoons, studying for her CDL, while I rolled around on the bed, working through practice tests for the GRE. I had moved out of my own apartment because my brother's room was free and my boyfriend Tom and I were fighting again.

Just a few days later, though, I was stacking my bras and underwear back into the top drawer of Tom's dresser, laughing. Our dramatic two-day separation had ended. As I turned toward the bedroom door, my eye caught something hanging on the wall that I didn't recognize. I squinted and walked to the head of the bed.

A banal four-by-six-inch photograph of a shoreline sunset was placed haphazardly above Tom's pillow. Our apartment décor was mostly dissected calendars hung up with sticky tack, so while the taped-up snapshot didn't seem particularly out of place, it was decidedly crooked. As I was examining the photo, wondering if Tom might have intended it to function as some sort of dream catcher, charm against insomnia, or, it vainly occurred to me, monument to loss, he came into the room.

"What's this?"

Tom's eyebrows shot up as he set his jaw. He looked down and in a voice I knew well—one so deliberately quiet, the suppressed sentiment was louder than it would have been had he shouted—said, "I punched a hole in the wall the other morning."

My mouth dropped open. "You punched a *hole* in the wall?"

Tom squirmed. "Yeah."

I reached toward the photograph and shoved one corner under my fingernail, then peeled it away from the wall. Tom had always prided himself on being a laid-back guy, but the fist-sized black spot above our bed suggested something different. No wonder he'd hastily pasted over it with a setting sun.

Looking at the ragged hole, I imagined a world of unseemly things living in the space behind the drywall. Termites, roaches, maybe even rats. Could something get out? Without asking Tom any further questions, I replaced the photograph as neatly as I could, straightening it, perhaps imperceptibly.

• • • • • • •

At the time, I was two years out of college and working three part-time jobs. One job was at Borders, stocking shelves early in the morning. After mom got beat up, I used my employee discount to buy a book called *The Domestic Violence Sourcebook* and then spent the next two nights carefully underlining sections that I knew applied to her. Under "emotional abuse," I underlined "forbidding someone to see friends or family," "hurting or threatening children or pets," and "refusing to help someone who is sick or hurt." I bracketed and put a star beside a bullet point that read: "In one study of violent homes, all sons over fourteen attempted to protect their mothers. Sixty-two percent were injured in the process. Another study found that 63 percent of the males between the ages of fifteen and twenty who are incarcerated for homicide killed their mother's batterer." I was worried how my brother might react. I was worried how *I* might react if I ever saw the man. I'd pointedly refused to meet him for months, suggesting what I thought was a reasonable ultimatum: "Tell him if he can keep a job, pay his child support, and not punch anyone for six months, I'll think about it."

I marked off sixteen of the twenty-five traits of an abusive man and traced question marks beside a few I thought were the case but hadn't heard stories confirming yet. Some passages got underlined, starred, and bracketed. Beside one passage, I drew a frowny face with two tears dropping from its left eye: "One action that does not help a battered woman is to push her or badger her to leave before she is ready." I'd been "badgering" Mom at every opportunity—

it seemed impossible not to. But the book seemed to suggest an apology was in order.

I sent the book off and was duly thanked, but I assumed Doug would be back.

THE SWEEPER

It was during a Doug reprieve that we were all introduced to the Filterqueen Majestic. After Mom had finished her demonstration, Carol obliged her by asking questions, and Mom threw phrases at us like, "Five-year bumper-to-bumper warranty" and "class II medical device," terminology that obviously came from the company script. Mom talked like she was carrying too much air in her lungs.

I assumed Carol was simply being agreeable and didn't want to spend over $1,000 on a fancy class-II medical device for sucking up cat hair. I went to the kitchen to look for something to eat.

Mom and Dad soon came in and started talking in hushed voices. Mom looked at Dad and quietly, quaveringly, with a fresh and fragile hope that would haunt me for years, asked, "Did I just make a sale?" Dad looked down and then up and then frowned and shook his head and said, "No, I don't think so."

"Damn," she said, dragging the word out for two beats.

Eventually, Carol rose stiffly from the couch to head back down the stairs. Then Mom picked up the phone and called in two orders. I listened as she bought one sweeper for herself and then one for a "man," a "Mr. . . . uh . . . Zaleski?" Her intonation rising, she pretended not to know my father.

•••••••

Mom really needed that third sale. She and Dad had dropped over two grand to get her two-thirds of the way to a new job, but without sweeper number three, there would be no commission check. A few days after my parents' optimistic purchases, I arrived at my uncle's house on the heels of another demonstration. My cousin Jen and her family were there too, and everyone was pretending to yell at Jen's three-year-old son for playing in the one clean spot of carpet in the house, the spot Mom had apparently just been sweeping. "No, don't play there! You'll get it dirty!" they laughed. My cousin's son, Jared, was running around the house, not paying them any mind.

Later, Jen called Jared over, bent down, and whispered in his ear. When she finished, Jared headed toward his grandpa. When Jared arrived at his predetermined stopping point, Jen provided the prompt—"Hey, Jared, what do you want from Grandpa for Christmas?"—and right on cue, he delivered his line, "A Majestic!"

"What?" my uncle laughed. "What do you want?"

Jared looked back at his mom, then turned and shouted, "A football!"

We all laughed, and no one bought a sweeper.

THE RESIDUE

In the months that followed, Mom would give up on cleaning and, having earned her CDL, drive across the country in a semi. She trained with a woman whose CB handle was Gypsy and who called out into the night, "This is Gypsy. I go and I go. To and fro. Where I'll stop, nobody knows."

It would in fact be Albuquerque where Gypsy stopped without warning, told Mom she didn't want to share her truck anymore, and left her stranded in the middle of the country. Mom called the company, and they told her to call Greyhound. And though she had been out of work for months, and though the company reassured her that she would be reimbursed, she had to buy the ticket herself. She came home, defeated, and got back together with Doug.

Tom and I finally broke up. In the final months, Tom spent more time scraping resin out of his bowl than grading student papers. When I complained about it, Mom latched onto Tom's trouble with marijuana and said, "An addict's an addict," which meant, *Tom's no different than Doug*. Which meant, *You're no different than me*. A few weeks after this conversation, Mom had major surgery while Doug was MIA. He returned to steal her Percocet.

Meanwhile, Dad moved out of the tiny upstairs apartment and bought a cavernous three-bedroom home. Living on his own for the first time in a family-sized house, he took his noble Filterqueen but rarely used it.

He made plans for a tattoo, a line drawing of a dove overlaid by the text, "If you love something, set it free. If it returns, it's yours forever. If not, it was never meant to be." When I asked him where he planned to get the tattoo, he named Hammers, a tattoo shop.

"No," I said. "Where on your body?"

"Oh." Over his heart of course.

The big, empty house grew dusty around him while he tested his proverb.

MOVING

I. THE STORY OF THE COUCH

It is easier to die than to move.
—Susan Burling Ward in Angle of Repose, *by Wallace Stegner*

I was one of those kids who moved a lot.

Then again, I wasn't.

Every few years, my parents angled the couches and mattresses down the hallways and staircases and jammed them into a borrowed pickup truck while we kids said goodbye to our favorite trees, hiding places, and pets buried in the backyard. Then we'd drive two minutes down the street and start our new life in the same small Ohio town.

My parents lived under the spell of two competing phobias: leaving the only town they'd ever known and dying there. Growing up, my siblings and I memorized a long string of house and phone numbers but only a handful of street names and one zip code, 44618. There were no real attractions to gravitate toward or commutes to avoid in 44618—you either were or were not close to the Hardee's.

When we weren't preparing to move into a new house, we were remodeling the current one. My Saturday morning alarm clock was sometimes the pounding of a sledgehammer. I'd drag myself to the kitchen and shove cereal into my mouth while Dad adjusted his neon-green safety glasses and took out some drywall. We kids were rarely consulted on these changes, which made sleepovers risky. I had a friend stay the night once, and he woke up to his bed shaking. He opened his eyes in the faint morning light, and there were my parents, whispering apologies and pushing his roll-away bed out of the living room and into the kitchen so they could chisel up the flooring.

Sometimes funds ran short, and we had to tolerate the same color of paint in the living room for multiple seasons. And occasionally, the will to finish a project stalled out, like the time we stripped the paneling off the kitchen walls, exposing a lime-green surface with gluey wrinkles, spackled all the holes, and then lost interest. I came home from school one day to find all of our pictures hung back up on the walls, as if that was how we intended them to look, as if spackle and glue were the newest trend in wall texturing.

But most days, my family was tearing up the floor we stood on. Back then I called it hope for something better.

• • • • • • •

The last move we made together was eighteen years ago. In one weekend, the five of us moved our belongings out of four separate houses spread across the state of Ohio and into one house in 44618. Like always, my parents' new house was only a few miles from the last one they'd lived in. My sister was moving back home temporarily before relocating to South Africa, and my brother and I were coming home from college.

The day started at U-Haul, where Dad rented the largest truck he could legally operate and then drove it down to Cincinnati, swinging through Columbus so my brother and I could follow him down I-71 in a car. We had decided to pack up my sister's apartment first because it presented the largest logistical challenge.

The problem waiting for us there was a green couch that was too gigantic to be escorted through the staircases, despite my sister's unhappy dog having gnawed away at it for months. In order to move the couch in, we'd had to rent a lift and guide the bulky piece of furniture through the living room bay window on the second story.

This time, impelled by the ingenuity a lack of money inspires, we decided to lasso the couch to my dad and sister, both strong and heavy, who would then lower it down to the outstretched arms of my brother and I, both tall, waiting below on the sidewalk. The lasso strategy was Dad's, which gave us reason to pause.

My father is an engineer by profession, but his plans for coordinating moving bodies outside of work typically turn out poorly: unmanned cars rolling down hills, boys on vines slamming into tree trunks, Mom screaming, "Aren't you a fucking engineer?" So to be safe, we first took my sister's mattress out to the street and leaned it up against a neighbor's truck parked in the couch's fallout zone. Then, slowly, the green fabric appeared over the lip of the windowsill, and the couch tipped farther and farther until it hung straight down. I pictured my dad and sister slipping on the dusty hardwood above and flying out the window after that heavy fabric counterweight, busting into a million pieces on the sidewalk, or perhaps landing graciously on the couch they were tethered to. But like most disasters you anticipate, this one didn't happen.

When my sister's house had been cleared, we drove to Columbus and, without incident, added my furniture and my brother's to the U-Haul. Finally, we arrived at my parents' new house and lay down on the living room carpet. Then Mom crawled over on all fours and told us to get back to work.

Mom hadn't been with us on the trip because of a back injury—she was scheduled for surgery and could barely walk. Instead she'd been crawling, and now there were blisters below her kneecaps, seeping with pus. No one was sure when the truck was due back, but Mom thought it was that night.

We started whining, and Mom started yelling.

In my family, the most successful form of argument is rage. When my mom yells, it's as if she rips herself in two and hurls words down from a mountain of flames and a storm cloud of tears. And as a defective vacuum cleaner once could have told you while flying off a second-story porch, she can be very persuasive.

Back at the foot of the ramp, I saw Mom crawling along the floor of the truck, moving freight. She would crawl up to a box and then put her bent right arm to its side. I'd hear her exhale and see the weighted cardboard skid a few feet across the metal floor. Then she'd crawl up to where it had stopped, cock her arm, and give it another shove. She sure seemed eager to start her new life in that same small town.

With Mom on all fours to goad us, the truck was soon empty and the basement filled to capacity with three houses' worth of furniture. There were two full bedroom suites, two kitchen tables, a mini-refrigerator and freezer, two cedar chests, three computer desks, and so on and sewing machines.

And I was there too: twenty-two and done with school, standing in my parents' basement. The house was, for once, incredible, and I thought Mom and Dad might happily retire there, with the front yard swooping down into a cow pasture and creek, the backyard fenced in by tall pines and a ravine.

That night, over pizza and orange Mountain Dew, I mentioned a job in Seattle. From across the room where Mom lay on the ground, only her sneakers visible through the forest of boxes, a voice called out, "I can't wait to get out of this town."

After pizza, Dad had to back the U-Haul down the steep driveway after attempting and failing a three-point turn eight times. Rounding a tight corner, he ran over some bushes as I spun my hands wildly in a circle, telling him to turn! Turn more!

In a rare moment that unified shouting and an accurate assessment of the situation, my dad yelled out the window, “You suck at giving directions!” as he roared off in the enormous truck.

I don’t deny it. I’ve never understood the physical laws predicting motion. If you ask me where a Hoover launched from a height of eight feet and traveling at a rate of twenty miles per hour will land, I’ll tell you the junkyard. But even harder to know are the human needs that move us—in circles, out windows, down paths devoid of logic.

2. THE STORY OF THE TUB

Since I’ve been able to write my name, my dad’s coached me on how to paint walls: tape around the vents and the ceiling, roll to the doorway, then use the brush to fill in the gap. When I was eight, my mom let us kids paint our bedroom furniture black and then add red spots with a can of spray paint. The design looked awful, and the drawers stuck.

Eighteen years ago, my parents moved into the house with the creek and the pasture, and we kids splintered off to opposite ends of the globe, intent on building adult lives. A year later, the strange, circular trail my parents had been making in 44618 turned sharply, anarchically. They divorced and moved into new towns with different zip codes, their destinations outliers in the pattern I’d been carefully plotting.

That last house in 44618, where we'd eaten pizza and drunk Mountain Dew, wasn't like the other houses my parents had lived in. It was too big, too well maintained—there was nothing to tear down. My parents trimmed a few trees and dumped chemicals in the pool. They Windexed the glass walls in the sunroom until the panels disappeared. They looked longingly at the living room walls, but the honey-toned wooden boards wouldn't bear paint. They scuffed their feet at the carpet; it was clean and soft. They looked down the sloping front yard and saw open pastures and a lawn thick as the hair on our heads. Nothing needed fixing. This was something new indeed.

Over the next months, my parents sent short updates across continents to us kids: The house is gorgeous. There is so much *room*.

Room enough for my sister's crazy dog to tear around in the fields until its life of neurotic apartment suffering melted away. Instead of socks, the dog chomped on groundhogs. My parents could even argue in the hot tub and not have the neighbors call the cops. What to do with all that freedom?

Mom and Dad sat on the wooden balcony and twiddled their thumbs. They concluded there was nothing to be done about the house. Then they took a long look at each other.

• • • • • • •

Meanwhile, my brother took my sister's couch and ruined it. Confounded by a narrow stairwell, he and his roommates initiated and then abandoned a plan to cut the behemoth in half. When I visited him a few months after he moved in, I found the couch still standing vertically in the landing right inside his front door, marked with gashes where he'd taken a saw to it.

I was saddened to witness the couch in such a state because I remembered the last time I had seen it, hanging above me. That day, the couch seemed a symbol, perhaps for how we managed: half of us waiting below with arms outstretched, some cumbersome thing we cherished suspended precariously but on its way toward us, and half of us two stories up, bound to the thing itself.

• • • • • • •

In the year or two following the divorce, my parents moved even more frequently. First Mom moved into an apartment in a small city near 44618, and then she bought a house in a town named Big Prairie. In Big Prairie, she lived across the road from the Ripley Church of Christ, which she called the Church of Ripley's Believe It or Not. I visited her at that house only a few times, and I mostly remember how at night, the fog lying over the field in front of the house looked like a black and green sea. I also remember the coffee maker on the counter and the cheap beer in the fridge—signs that her boyfriend had made himself at home. After a few months, she lost the house and bought a one-bedroom trailer in a place called Sterling.

Dad moved out of the house on the hill and took over the lease on the apartment Mom had first rented. Eventually, he bought a place that had been sitting vacant for two years, a three-bedroom with a lot of storage, so the few boxes of belongings my siblings and I still hadn't the room for landed at his place. So did we, when we visited "home." Mom took our staying at Dad's as a sign that we didn't like her, but really, we were avoiding the boyfriend—who was always in and out because he hit her—and a weekend sleeping on a couch.

When I was in the area and Mom's boyfriend wasn't, I'd go over to her trailer to eat supper. After supper I would keep snacking, and a pile of dishes would stack up by the sink. She sometimes seemed relieved to have something to clean.

Dad was lost without Mom, and at the age of forty-seven, he fought through nausea to addict himself to cigarettes. He thought them a necessary fixture for anyone whose mood was as black as his. The walls in the bedrooms upstairs had only a coat of primer, but he showed no interest in painting them or fixing the hole in the kitchen ceiling where water had burst through.

Though Mom felt guilty about it, she let Dad come over and fix things in her trailer when they broke, either through simple wear or because her boyfriend had broken them. Once, the broken object was a lawn mower. Once, an air conditioner. Once, the controller on his and Mom's old sleep number bed that someone else now slept in.

I watched Dad repair that controller. He seemed relieved to have something he could fix and ecstatic that it was for her. Perhaps, I thought as I observed Dad disassemble the little box, desire is a thing best kept under a roof and between four visible walls, its only object concrete, breakable, remake-able.

In the bathroom of that perfect house where my parents' marriage tumbled to pieces, a beautiful, cream-colored clawfoot tub sat immaculate and unused. My parents should have painted it black, with red spots.

3. THE STORY OF THE WELL

For years I had been writing about that green couch, making claims about what it meant, most of which were easy and pretty to say but only a little true. It seemed there was no getting the story right, given the way we were all still moving around the edges.

For a time, Mom and Dad continued as they were, Mom dating an addict and Dad moping and waiting, biding his time. They saw each other at least once a week for the solemn exchanging of the dogs, a pseudo-shared custody arrangement involving one fluffy mutt and one golden retriever.

My parents seemed ready to stay put—and apart. Then, perhaps tired of the continually shifting housing arrangements his erratic behavior precipitated, Mom's boyfriend got himself arrested for cooking meth and found permanent housing in prison.

She lived alone for some time, enough time, after that. In the front yard of her trailer was a wishing well that had followed her from the last house in 44618 to the lost house in Big Prairie. She dissembled it and then burned it to the ground.

Dad didn't put his lonely house up for sale immediately but did so inevitably. When it sold, Dad gave half of his bachelor housewares and furniture to the young family next door, and Mom let him move into the trailer with her. The trailer was so small, they didn't have much to work on. A new period of stillness followed as my parents considered making peace with what abided in each of them.

Then they got moving again.

I can't remember where I was living when my parents remarried each other, though I know by then I was in my thirties. If I wanted to, I could figure it out—ask them the year and then count back my moves—but leaving the date imprecise feels right, as we children were not there. Instead, Mom and Dad sent us an email the day after: "We know you are all very busy and felt it best to wait to tell you afterwards. Sorry if that wasn't cool."

No one was surprised by this development, given our family's knack for repeatedly moving nowhere. My parents weren't even the first couple in the extended family to reunite after a divorce. My aunt Kay and uncle Greg, my uncle Dan and aunt Rose—all of them ended things only to get right back together again.

Mom and Dad bought a house outside Akron, their second house on a hill. Most of the original major structures were right on the brink of failure—within two years, my parents would replace the roof, the furnace, the air conditioner, the hot water heater, and the water filtration system. Then they went to work on the interior, on the porch, on the four-acre wooded property. They built a new retaining wall, cleared poison ivy, felled dead trees, and hauled a tacky decorative outhouse to the dump.

Over time, the projects started to move beyond the realm of necessity. One weekend when I was visiting, Dad set his heart on pulling a detached vertical pipe out of an abandoned well. With the pipe out, the well could be filled, the concrete cap removed, and grass seed planted over top. I was unenthusiastic about the project, and after peering down the full length of the lead drop pipe, about twenty feet down with a submersible pump still attached, expressed doubt that it was feasible with just the three of us.

Nonetheless, we gathered ropes, tie straps, and winches, crouched at the mouth of the well—backs bent, hands stacked—and pulled. The pipe came up about a foot. We took turns shifting our grips down around the two-inch diameter and pulled again. The pipe rose another foot.

After a few more pulls, we had about seven feet of pipe out of the well. Now we paused to reassess, while bit by bit, the strength in our hands and arms drained along the empty tube.

"Can we tie it off now?" someone asked. "Could we cut it here?"

"Ropes aren't going to hold it, it's way too heavy," someone else, probably me, said.

"Try it anyway."

Haphazardly, I wrapped and knotted the ropes, trying to make fast work of it while Mom and Dad stood bracing the pipe.

We pulled some more, panting now. The awkward topside half of the pipe began to wobble from side to side. We had to make a decision: keep heaving together or see if the ropes held. The well was too narrow to angle the pipe past its downward return trajectory and into a tilt toward the ground. We decided the ropes would slip.

We all tremored as fatigue coupled with doubt and frustration. My dubious heart pumped furiously. Dad held fast to his reckless faith and yelled at us to *lift*! Mom angrily obliged, unconvinced but willing to try. I pulled one last time with what I knew was no longer my full effort, my will run dry.

"It's not going to work!" I yelled. "This is stupid!"

We stood in exhausted silence, hating everything.

"Someone is going to get hurt," Mom said.

We were too deep into the problem now to easily disengage, to simply throw up our hands and drop it. The ropes would have to be untied, and then we would have to let go together and leap away as the hundred-pound pipe fell back down the length of our wasted efforts.

The most useless stay against the pipe's gravity, I was allowed to let go again in order to untie the ropes. We counted down, and then we leapt. The pipe sank out of sight, clanking down to thud in a little deeper than where it had started.

We took a second to look ourselves over and found we had emerged relatively unscathed, with all our fingers attached and our faces unsmashed. Soon, though, Mom lay down stiffly on the ground and blew out a long breath. She rubbed her side. "Goddamn it. I think I threw my back out."

Gathered on a different sloping front yard beside a hole in the ground, we were not exactly the same people who had tied ourselves to a couch or spun our hands ineffectually in circles or pushed boxes on our knees several years ago. Not quite, though the resemblance was striking. One of us, at least, had grown, though on this day she had been dragged to the ground on a fool's errand. Dad would later say it was a day of masculine overestimation. Certainly it was a day in which we asked for too much and forgot that sometimes, in home improvement, you must abandon the ideal change for the acceptable.

The well was later backfilled by a professional team, who plugged the gaping hazard and sealed off the groundwater access point. They said the pipe could stay put, so now it is all one submerged tube of solid material, a deep, sturdy spike in the middle of the soft earth. Who knows how long it will hold its form—long enough perhaps for knowledge of its existence to slip away, until one day far in the future, an excavation clangs up hard against it. We do not worry about these future excavators, and they will know nothing of us, our exasperation and then acquiescence in letting the deepest problems lie.

4. THE STORY OF THE PERENNIALS

We have lived too shallowly in too many places.
—Lyman Ward in Angle of Repose, *by Wallace Stegner*

I am now forty-one years old and have received mail at twenty-three US postal addresses. As an adult, the longest I had lived at any one residence, until recently, was two years.

After I finished graduate school, I took a job in the middle of the country, drove a thousand miles, and then walked up two flights of stairs into an inexpensive apartment I had rented unseen. Inside, in a futile last-minute gesture, the landlord was laying linoleum.

Of the many subpar sublets and apartments I had bedded down in, this was to be among the worst. Cigarette burns in carpet I had been told would be new, a weekly trek to the laundromat despite optimistic projections of on-site appliances, a woodblock laminate countertop that spoke to me of desolation reaching back to the seventies. The landlord sent me rude text messages and screamed at other tenants.

In all my years of renting, I had known but two good landlords. Max, the man who owned the farmhouse in which I spent my elementary school years, charged us so little to reside there, in the childhood home of his late wife, that my father said he had subsidized our childhood. When my parents made improvements, he accepted receipts in lieu of payment. And once, a lovely couple I rented from in Tucson shocked me to my core by handing me a key to a freshly cleaned studio apartment.

In my third-floor one-bedroom in the middle of the country, I lay on the couch listening to an air conditioner that blew, but only metaphorically, and an ear-piercing freezer rattle. I was done with school—really, truly done this time—and I had a job with no foreseeable termination date. I was certainly tired of running the rental gamut. Under the permanent cloud that loomed over my deposits, for fifteen years, I had never had the courage to tap a nail into the wall. Maybe, I thought, it was time to own my own piece of shit.

I applied to a program for low-income, first-time homeowners and was accepted. The program aimed to rehabilitate homes in depressed neighborhoods and settle them with long-term residents. In exchange for agreeing to sit through several courses on responsible homeownership, I qualified for a $20,000 loan toward closing costs and repairs deemed necessary by the organization, half forgivable over ten years if I stayed put.

I found a small house in need of large repairs and bought it for a low price. Then I called my parents.

• • • • • • •

Before my parents arrived, I cleaned. The previous owner of the house was in his nineties and had not been able to keep up with it for some time. On the hard surfaces of the kitchen and bathroom, the neglect was caked in layers, and I took the blade from a box cutter and sheared off the gunk. I recycled and wiped and sanded and scrubbed. I scoured the forgotten refrigerator top and dislodged pink salt granules from cupboard corners, readying the bare space for a set of objects I hoped would rest there a long time.

When my parents arrived, dressed in raggedy paint clothes and sweatbands, they mowed through tasks in wide swaths. Patching and painting walls, polishing brass hardware, replacing P-traps and wall sockets. Their expert forward progress was a marvel to behold. They stayed less than a week and then drove the fourteen hours home on a Saturday. Monday morning, when Mom clocked in at the warehouse, her coworkers asked about her trip. Looking at her bone-weary face, one asked, "Where'd you go on vacation—hell?"

• • • • • • •

In a world of six of one, half dozen of the other, owning a home is to decidedly hold at least seven things. I still had loud neighbors, but now they were two houses over, not on the other side of a wall. My misanthropy waned in proportion to my distance from other people.

The house was shady with old flowerbeds in which the gravel mulch, over decades, had sunk back into the earth. I began the process of digging it out, straining it through chicken wire over a wheelbarrow, and dumping the loose dirt back in place. I started walking the neighborhood and ogling my neighbor's plants. I spent long nights reading about hardy perennials and soon realized I had developed a full-blown hobby. Me, an inveterate grump, plotting a future in flowers.

My second year, I started filling in the beds, foot by foot, month by month, season by season. A summer wine ninebark and a purple pearl beautyberry. Lungwort and spiderwort and sem sorbaria. Brunnera, feathergrass, and angelina sedum. I agonized over depth, surprised by how difficult it could be to dig and fill a hole that left a sizeable root ball just above ground level, and at least once, I had an overnight crisis of faith that led to a wholesale disgorgement and transplant the next day, an act that felt deranged and violent. *God, I have killed it!* I thought a dozen times that summer. On hot days, I went into the yard after work and drug my hose along the line slowly, placing the nozzle at the base of each plant and letting it trickle for a minute at a time. Come fall, I threw down my mulch and hoped.

•••••••

When spring came, I made daily rounds and examined the dirt and the twiggy shrubs for signs of growth, convinced all the plants had gone under in a permanent winter die-off. Maybe I hadn't watered enough. Maybe I had watered too much. Maybe the mulch was too shallow. Maybe the mulch was too deep.

A family tale, like an untended garden, can grow into an unwieldy thing. I know this one has. Its younger self went out into the world only three parts long, and before that, for years, I thought it finished first with one and then two. But it just keeps growing, every conclusion partial, every lesson unfinished. To stay or move on, tear down or hold steady, to muzzle the heart's clamor with distractions or to sit still and listen. Today, I am remaking the story again, both grateful for the wear and tear that keeps me busy and wary of stopping. But that spring, for the first time, when the leaves shot out green, I was standing over them, watching what can happen when you let the roots run deep.

WITH MEANING

WAKING UP IS HARD TO DO

Off in a lab somewhere, a sad mouse is swimming. He's stuck in a beaker half full of water, and claw all he wants, he can't get a purchase on the glass. His back paws punch the water, alternating in rapid succession, so it looks like he's wagging his tail.

Really, the mouse is drowning.

When he reaches the point where he's nearly spent, the point where a happier mouse would redouble his efforts and make one final surge for the rim, the sad mouse simply stops swimming—says *fuck it* and sinks to the bottom. Thinks: *Eh. Life wasn't that great anyway*. This is how the researchers know he's depressed.

In my twenties, I frequently could not get out of bed. Mornings when I didn't have any obligations beyond exchanging carbon dioxide for oxygen, I felt like a sad lab mouse. When I reached the point of semiconsciousness, the point at which a happier person would open her eyes and swim through the four minutes of groggy discomfort in order to fully awaken and start living, I tucked my head under the sea of covers and went down for the count. *Ah, fuck it,* I said. *Life just isn't that interesting.* I was down for a long time too—six, eight, ten hours, this after the eight I'd already gotten when I elected to sink instead of swim. This is how I knew I was depressed.

Too much or too little sleep: both are symptoms of depression. I often wished I erred on the side of insomnia because I was delusional about how productive I'd be during all those extra hours. Sometimes I told people sleeping was my superpower and then tried to think up scenarios in which hypersomnia would save the day. I couldn't think of any.

Once fully awake, if I happened to go horizontal, standing back up was often an insurmountable challenge. If the lights were on, I could not traverse the two and a half feet from my bed to the switch. If I was so dehydrated that swallowing was painful, my efforts to rehydrate stopped at parched longing. I even had a recurring daydream in which I rigged a hamster water bottle up over the bed—then all I'd have to do was extend my tongue. Countless nights and mornings a glass of water sitting only an arm's reach away conquered me. *Even if I manage to reach it,* I thought, *then I'd have the trouble of lifting up my head to drink.* In the fight to remain motionless, my will was indomitable.

Even when my depression is well managed, as it is now, waking up is the hardest thing I do all day. Inertia is part of the challenge, as the transition from object at rest to object in motion is always an uncomfortable one, even law-defying. Once I'm upright, everything else feels simple by comparison. But I'm also battling the deep animal pleasure of half-sleep. Imagine you are getting a massage and the masseuse suddenly asks, "Are you ready for me to stop so that you can walk over a long patch of gravel to sit in front of a TV playing a bad sitcom?" Most days, that's what the proposition of waking up sounds like. When I don't have much that needs doing, staying in bed feels as logical as it does sensual, and it feels really good.

My mouth is better at starting the day than the rest of me. When I worked the early shift at a café, Pop-Tarts were crucial in getting me out from under the ten tons of existential resignation piled on my chest. I kept a box of the pastries on the bookshelf beside my bed. When my alarm went off, with my eyes still closed, I'd reach out, unwrap a packet of Pop-Tarts, and cram one between my teeth. Sure as a Honda, my credulous mouth would start up, convinced by the frosting and sprinkles that the world held only good things for it that day. Eventually, the rest of me would follow my mouth into action, if not optimism.

•••••••

These days, I typically get a healthy nine hours of sleep a night, and when I tell people this, they inevitably say, "God, I *wish* I could get that much sleep." But nine hours is no more than the upper threshold of what is recommended: seven to nine. Some of these people, I know, have trouble falling asleep and staying asleep, and others have two jobs and two children and any other number of sleep-limiting responsibilities. My mother wakes up at the crack of dawn every day and can't go back to sleep, and my sister has a full-time job and a ten-year-old. But many of the people I know getting five to six hours of sleep a night are relatively young and unfettered, and these people are tired for no good reason.

"I'm so *tired*," they say. Why? "Netflix." Then they tip back a five-dollar latte and go on about their day.

I am also one of those intolerable people who doesn't drink coffee, partly out of annoyance with the cutesy way caffeine addiction is celebrated. Instead, I stumble through the morning, half-human for half an hour.

I hate waking up because once the process begins in earnest, my peaceful awareness of rest abruptly becomes an intense experience of tiredness, and I *hate* feeling tired. That waking up involves feeling tired may seem obvious, but I almost never feel tired once I get going, and not all people feel tired when they wake up. I briefly dated a man who hadn't set an alarm in years. Every day around 6 a.m., even in the depths of a Midwestern winter, he simply woke the fuck up. Watching him rise noiselessly and get dressed in the shadows was like witnessing a miracle.

Though neurologists of sleep have made progress toward disentangling moral judgments from one's status as an early bird or a night owl, smugness appears to be an unavoidable side effect of waking up early. I know this because I am a night owl who occasionally joins running groups, and one week into rising any time before 7 a.m., my sense of superiority over those still in bed is insufferable even to me. But good evidence exists that like so many aspects of human experience, natural variations in sleep patterns are standard fare. The irony is that my fellow late risers don't seem satisfied with the equal standing lent us by these studies, which investigate topics like delayed sleep phase syndrome and the negative impact of too-early school start times on the cognitive development of children. Sucked through the ego vortex of social media, the tentative conclusions of science morph into linked articles posted by otherwise reasonable friends at 3 a.m.: "Good News from Science: Night Owls Are Smarter and More Creative."

At the end of the day—or rather, the beginning—I'd rather wake up early. But I can only do that if other people are relying on me. For a year in college, I was on the women's crew team, and I had to wake up before 5 a.m. to get to practice. I was the stroke of an eight, which meant I set the pace for seven other women, who followed my rhythm. I was not the best technical rower, and I wasn't the strongest. I didn't even work the hardest. That honor belonged to Sarah, who pulled so hard she broke her own ribs—twice. But what I did better than anyone else was follow instructions. When the coxswain said take it down to thirty-eight strokes per minute, that's what my body did—no faster, no slower. Never mind that the initial adrenaline sometimes makes it hard for a stroke to keep the pace slow enough and that the pain eventually makes it very hard to keep the pace fast enough. Even then, at nineteen—rowing backward down the river like a metronome—I thought, there's something strange about the way my will works: it listens to everyone but me.

• • • • • • •

I don't especially believe in willpower. Best-selling pop psychology and neurology books like *Blink* and *Incognito* also tell us to be skeptical. So does a psychology PhD student I once knew who first learned how to boil water on a stove around the same time his lab was generating rat-based data suggesting free will was an illusion. He was my friend's housemate, and my friend was disturbed by the claims he was making. To me, the rat hypothesis sounded similar to what Benjamin Libet found while watching the brains of people who were asked to move their hand whenever they felt like it. After analyzing patterns of electrical activity, Libet noticed that these volitional acts were always "preceded by a specific electrical change in the brain." The participants reported becoming aware of their intention *after* this change but before the act itself. Libet concluded that "the volitional process is therefore initiated unconsciously." Though the decision to move seemed made *for* the hand movers rather than *by* the hand movers, Libet also found that the decision to move could be consciously "vetoed." What this suggests for the concept of free will is that we can't consciously initiate actions, but we can decide *not* to act on the promptings our unconscious suggests.

This finding makes sense to me and helps me understand what I do and what I don't do—two categories that hardly break down logically. Getting two master's degrees required nothing that felt like drive, resolve, or even effort. Sometimes I felt as if I'd simply been manufactured to go to graduate school. A class was scheduled, and before I understood what was happening, my body had transported me to the classroom. A paper was due, and by some genetic sorcery, I was suddenly reading far more scholarship than was necessary and then turning it in, on time, for an A.

Of course there are practical reasons for turning in homework. I sailed along on university ships—scholarships, fellowships, assistantships—for a decade because I always did well in school. There was also the avoidance of shame. Mostly, though, I did it because an authority figure physically present in my life required it of me. Whether from my unconscious, a teacher, or a boss, orders that originate in something not recognizably me are the easiest to follow.

This is why six extra years of college proved far less challenging than drinking six glasses of water a day. True, nameless, faceless authorities tell me I must drink six to eight glasses of water a day, but they're distant enough that making this commitment always feels self-willed. By day two of my vigilant hydrating, I'm haunted by the image of an ocean of tap water spread out before me—an ocean that I have taken upon myself to swallow, six glasses at a time. The vision is too much to bear.

If I have to try—in other words, when an action feels hard—I will eventually fail. Trying is the thing I do before giving up. Diets are a good example. When I go on a diet, I make sure to eat a bunch of crap first. I walk around the kitchen downing Little Debbie oatmeal creme pies as if they were potato chips, a one-person Fat Tuesday parade.

This is what trying with food looks like: first, I obsessively plan meals to balance my macro- and micronutrient intake, then I go vegan, then I go raw, then I buy a $150 juicer and liquefy $160 worth of produce over the course of three days. Then I damn it all to hell. I don't so much fall off the horse as eat so much the horse breaks a leg. Once down, I've found that adding tuna to my boxed macaroni and cheese adds nuanced undertones to the flavor of my failure.

At other times, healthy food consistently finds its way into my body through no discernable exertion of will. In the last ten years (and here I borrow a joke from an old boss), I have lost over ninety pounds—the same thirty pounds three times.

• • • • • • •

In my fourth year of graduate school, just before the days of far too much sleep set in, I voluntarily underwent my own version of the mouse's forced swimming test. I was not in a beaker of water but a pool, and I was not being tested by researchers in lab coats but a man wearing a Speedo and a whistle. In fact, the test was not set up to measure my relative state of hopelessness at all, just my swimming endurance. Given who I am, though, most tasks are an indicator of my relative hopelessness. Flossing, for example, correlates with my mood and the weather. The flossing often stops around December, and when I suddenly start up again, I know spring is coming.

Conditioned by team sports, I also can't exercise unless someone is blowing a whistle at me. Because I follow commands at the sound of a whistle the way Pavlov's dogs drooled over bell chimes, I enrolled in a college-level phys. ed. class and subjected myself to the authority of the instructor.

I have never been an especially strong swimmer. My parents have a video of me as a kid racing my cousins across a pool. Kicking my legs was an option that must not have occurred to me, because the whole way across, they're stuck out stiffly behind me, about a foot apart at the toes. Meanwhile I'm thrashing my arms against the water so violently it's as if I think this action—smashing the entire length of my arm against the surface of the water as hard as I can—is the primary mechanism of propulsion. My face is submerged for the length of the race, and this makes my efforts seem that much more earnest, that much more ridiculous. I look both utterly insane and utterly convinced that this is how one swims. When my face does come out of the water, I look surprised I haven't won.

My swimming had gotten slightly better over the course of the class, but only slightly. In order to get an A on the endurance test, I needed to swim twelve continuous minutes of front crawl, the stroke better known as "freestyle." Prior to that day, the longest I had continuously swum the front crawl was two minutes.

The question of whether I would do it or not—the question I dread having to answer every morning when it's time to get out of bed—never occurred to me. Not only was the twelve minutes of continuous front crawl for school—for a *grade*—but there was also a barefoot, potbellied man holding a clipboard on the pool deck ordering me to do it. When he blew his whistle, I swam. Back and forth. Back and forth.

At eight minutes, I started to feel tired. Instead of pulling my arms down across my body, I started slipping into my old windmill stroke, which, because it generates so little power, uses up less energy. At ten minutes, I was not so much swimming as delaying drowning. I pushed on, not because I wanted to prove to myself that I could, but because it was required of me. I was not going to stop.

I didn't stop. I made it to the twelve-minute mark and then slapped my way down the lane to the wall. With my noodly arms shaking, I raised myself out of the pool. Then I stood dripping on the tile, coughing and panting my way down to a normal heart rate.

I got my A and didn't exercise for the next five years. Two decades out from my organized sports days, I still struggle to work exercise into my daily life. Of course, I didn't exercise back then either. I just went to practice.

• • • • • • •

Despite my preference for sleeping in, my medically attenuated depression, and my admission of sometimes feeling as if I have no willpower, I have always been a relatively high-achieving person with a substantial work output. I was one of two high school valedictorians, but I wasn't only studious—I also had the most varsity letters in my class. What a champ!

Volleyball was my least lettered and worst sport, which was unfortunate, as it was the school's best. Our coach had an incredible win-loss record, and in addition to the physical drills he made us practice, he expected us to exercise our minds and spirits. On Wednesdays, he sent us home with a typed-up half sheet titled "Mental Practice," which consisted of visualization tasks, like imagining in minute detail your execution of a perfect serve or pass.

I had no trouble visualizing success, but where I ran into trouble was in the celebration of success. Like most coaches, ours was obsessed with positivity, and he expected all of us to mark every point with almost hysterical exuberance. We had a collection of cheers, tailored to the occasion, which we coordinated and performed on court after every successful volley.

I loved my teammates, I loved competition, and I loved winning, but when I cheered, I was told, something about my face and body language failed to convey this. I remember my coach, who was also the principal, calling me into his office one day to talk about my undemonstrative nature and its negative effect on morale. Enthusiasm was infectious, but evidently I had a very strong immune system.

At a tournament one summer, in an echoic gym with empty bleachers, I remember a rare moment when I found myself the only one on the bench clapping after we'd scored a point. As the reverberations of my singular effort faded, I decided to kid my teammates sitting beside me. I started to ask them a question, and as the words came out of my mouth, I noticed they were devoid of intonation. In flatline monotone, I asked, "Am I the only one on this team with any enthusiasm?"

When I first started teaching college, we were assigned to film and review one of our own class sessions. My friend sat in the back with the camcorder while I made a conscious effort to appear animated. I smiled, told a few well-received jokes, and concluded I had put on a marvelous performance. In my head, my explanations of ethos and pathos rose and fell as mellifluously as the words of Winnie-the-Pooh. But when it came time to review the tape, the hilly contours were nowhere to be found, my voice following an unending plateau. I had been Eeyore all along.

Enthusiasm, I've noticed, is usually gendered female. All women get told to smile, and when I wear a dress or skirt, I am constantly told to cheer up. When I wear pants, though, the androgynous fashion choice mixes with my size and my mellow delivery such that sometimes, blessedly, people don't even notice that I'm a girl. Instead I'm just a human, plodding through the world.

•••••••

Around the same time I started working on the first draft of this essay, a draft on which I'd later leave a note for revision encouraging myself to "make the voice less psychotically depressed," I also signed up for a pottery class at a community arts center. I often felt like an alien watching another species build a civilization: *So they just make things out of clay? Because they want to?* I looked at the blob of dirt in front of me and tried to imagine myself working it into a form based solely on an ineffable desire moving through me.

I later realized while rooting through childhood memorabilia that the objects I fired were strikingly similar to some I had made in elementary school, only less interesting. The slab pitcher I made in the adult workshop was glazed a tan color and had three circles painted on the outside—one white, one yellow, one blue. On the outside of the one I'd made as a kid, I stuck a moon, a dolphin, a clump of seaweed, and an impressively rendered, three-dimensional blue octopus. How much time, I wonder, did I spend rolling out and attaching those octopus arms?

I am well enough to reliably get out of bed now, but that hasn't changed my basic constitution. I do plenty of things that look like they require willpower, but yardwork and half marathons and writing still mostly grow out of a sense of responsibility and curiosity. I still wake late, I still move slowly, and I still sound like I'm being sarcastic even when I don't intend to be.

At the end of my talk with the volleyball coach, in which he was perfectly kind, he said he hoped someday I would look back at our time together and think of him as a good coach who gave me some useful advice for the road ahead. He was certainly a good coach, but the advice he gave me didn't take. I still can't fake enthusiasm to save my life. So, if I ever really am drowning, I hope I swim like I did at seven. Insane, earnest. Wholly inept and wholly convinced I'll make it.

PRETTY DEAD THINGS

. . . as though any material were fit to receive man's stories.
—Roland Barthes

The summer after I received my first degree in English, I took a job as a kayaking guide on a Seattle lake twenty-five hundred miles from home. A week in I was joined by my boyfriend, Tom, who was nine years older, had three degrees in English, and was accustomed to having the summer off. As soon as we could, we set off to explore the coast, where almost immediately we came upon a curiously undead dead animal.

When Tom first saw the sea otter, he thought it was a bleached-out log like the ones we were gathering to build a fire. But as he reached for it, he saw this log had teeth, flipper feet, and a four-inch stick of penis. He called me over to look.

I was honestly stumped, unsure whether the otter was a mummy—some dried-out dead thing not decaying—or a sculptor's prank. To me, the tiny claws embedded in the toes looked just like grains of rice, the left whiskers like two dead pine needles. Conceivably, someone had sat on the beach and fashioned it.

Hanging around my neck was a new camera, so I decided to put it to work in resolving the problem: if the otter wasn't already art, I would simply make it so. I took thirteen pictures, framing the otter with the logs it resembled, isolating the webbed feet, rolling it over and recording how the stones left deep impressions in the flesh.

At home I opened the files on my computer screen and quickly found a favorite, an image in which the waning sunlight slants across the otter's face like a stalled tide. I was thrilled, the means of preservation now clarified.

•••••••

I passed most of my days that summer on the lake, playing tugboat to a flotilla of spent children. Tom occasionally picked up odd jobs—temporary manual labor positions like feeding unsalable Goodwill apparel into a baler. Mostly, though, he wandered. On one trip, he took my camera and returned to the coast, hiking, scrabbling over rocks for miles. Then, in a long, flat stretch of beach, an intensifying stench materialized into the corpse of a whale. I marveled at the pictures he brought home. The whale stretched over twenty feet, and I could see barnacles, baleen, and—peeking out of deep fissures—blubber. Gas pressure had blown open the ventral side, and guts spilled out like a cubic yard of sausages. There was no question whether this animal was rotting.

Still, far removed from the rocky coast, I cropped and edited the gore until I had made the whale a pretty dead thing, the second in my growing collection. How neatly it fit between the lines—a great dead beast tossed onto the edge of a continent—scalable from thumbnail to full screen.

•••••••

Now everywhere I looked, there were wasting bodies to resurrect: a tooth-torn spotted seal pup, a twisted gray bird on a gray beach, a tumbleweed of white feathers and bones beside a desert lake, a mess of rabbit torso and fluff under the wary eye of a crow. I walked in the company of sincere and unsubtle ideas.

Near the end of the summer, Tom received a letter of acceptance from a prestigious literary magazine and a promise of future payment. I continued to earn money by exhorting people in kayaks to "Paddle on the left! The left! The other left!" while they, steadily and inevitably, as if guided by a faulty homing device, drifted away from open water and toward the million-dollar yachts moored beyond our deck.

Eventually, though, the weather cooled, the crowds on the dock thinned, and my guide position ended, so Tom and I packed up the car and set out ourselves, back to Ohio.

• • • • • • •

We made a long and meandering trip of it, stopping to see the redwoods and sequoias, Reno, Tahoe, Yosemite, and the La Brea Tar Pits' sinking mammoth tableau. Then on to Death Valley, Zion, the Grand Canyon, and the Painted Desert. From there, we hit I-40 and drove hard. I remember we were in Oklahoma, among fields of white windmills, when we blew past a heap of densely muscled, auburn roadkill.

I knew it was unlikely, but to me the animal looked like a mountain lion. I appealed to Tom and convinced him to turn the car around. The cat's bad fortune seemed my good luck: an opportunity to capture a cougar, cat of many names and few sightings. It would be a fitting end, I decided, to my collection. While Tom drove along a one-lane dirt road parallel to the highway, I opened the sunroof, planted my feet on the passenger's seat, and stood scouting the berm like a guide on a macabre safari.

We parked, and I snapped a shot from the car. In the photo, the body resembles a giant cat, but the head looks too long, too narrow. Tom and I approached the carcass, only then noticing a pink band cinched around its neck. Dried streams of blood clogged the highway rumble strips, and like the whale, this animal's insides lay jumbled outside its skin.

But unlike the whale, whose exoticism tipped easily into the portentous, the crushed dog was not a pretty dead thing at all. I stood back from the prosaic highway mangling, impositions undone, and then fled.

• • • • • • •

We drove through the night, talking about the dog and our lingering unease. Tom, who was older and wiser and less surprised by the uncomfortable lesson I'd just had in my own conceit, tried a story from his undergraduate days in Wisconsin. Once, he said, during a particularly bad ice storm, a group of students traveling back to the school were killed in a car accident.

Our car hummed on while bugs burst unceremoniously on the windshield.

The campus was small, and the news spread quickly—over phones and across tables and in clouds of breath mingled with cigarette smoke. No one was untouched by grief. Unsure what to do with themselves, Tom and his friends wandered out into the woods. There, the glassy tree branches glinted in the moonlight and clacked in the wind. "And at some moment," he said, "I remember the mood shifted from mourning to a deep thankfulness for being alive. It was beautiful."

And then my body was flying forward into my seatbelt as he stomped on the brake, but he hit the house cat anyway—two loud *thunks* I felt in my stomach. The electric fear obliterated all ideas, our crafty symbols squashed so thoroughly by our own spinning wheels that I could barely claim the irony.

We had killed the cat with comic timing, the deadly thuds a resounding "no" to the question of whether the world, in its living and dying, had any interest in our stories.

But even this conclusion, I know, betrays my readiness for interpretation, the smudges of my vain tinkering. The drive for meaning is a hard one to break—we flattened a cat and haven't stopped yet.

ROMANTIC DESTINATIONS

My professed future plans when I graduated from high school were to become a wildlife biologist and study desert elephants in Namibia. I first did a year of biology coursework, and then, as a logical second step, I went to Costa Rica to save the sea turtles.

Informing this decision was a lot of television. In the late nineties and early aughts, I watched almost nothing on TV but Animal Planet. If you were to extrapolate based on Animal Planet footage, you might think the oceans are so stuffed with life you could walk from New Jersey to Spain on the backs of whales. Just float a little boat off the shore of South Africa, these shows suggest, and within minutes you'll be surrounded by great white sharks rocketing through the sky, chomping seals out of thin air.

I traveled with a group called International Student Travel (IST), which organized trips for college students combining two weeks of international conservation and community development with two weeks of ecotourism. One group would build Habitat houses, my group would steward turtle eggs, and then we'd all reunite in San José for the adventure half of the vacation, which was, in a word, comprehensive—ziplining across the rainforest, rappelling down waterfalls, kayaking through the mangroves, snorkeling in the Pacific, rafting the Pacuare, spotting quetzals in La Selva, and soaking in the hot springs of Arenal.

Before setting off, we had a two-day orientation at a Miami hotel. For our one-night stay, we shared hotel beds with other randomly assigned same-sex group members. Paranoid of imposing on a stranger, I made extra room for my sleeping partner by lying on my back at the far edge of the bed and demoting my outside leg to the floor. When I headed to the bathroom in the morning and transferred my weight onto a leg that had gone numb, I fell flat on my face and woke everyone with my laughter.

From Miami we flew to San José, and from San José my group bumped through a long van ride to the Gandoca-Manzanillo National Wildlife Refuge on the Caribbean coast. Over the noise of rubber on packed dirt, a girl named Aurora said she wanted to become a travel writer and read her first impressions aloud to us from her journal: "If Eskimos have a hundred words for snow, Costa Ricans must have a hundred for green."

Of course, I didn't know any better myself, wouldn't learn until the next year back at school that "Eskimos have a hundred words for snow" is in fact a well-received myth, but I was already willing to roll my eyes at Aurora and her friend Dustin. They were obviously sleeping together but were also loud advocates for free love and John Mayer.

When we arrived in Gandoca, we split off into smaller groups of roommates based on whatever affinities and aversions we'd developed in Miami and the van. Karen, a world-champion Irish dancer from Chicago, seemed laid-back. So did Jacqlyn, the marathon runner from Santa Barbara. Vanessa was reserved, and Holly, who'd had the bad luck of experiencing a ruptured stye a few days before we all met, had a black eye. I ended up with Karen, which I took as a good sign.

All the volunteers were hosted by local families, whom we paid for food and lodging. The only other viable source of income in

Gandoca was the banana plantation, whose pesticides were linked to increasing rates of cancer and infertility in the community. And so Karen and I lugged our bags out of the van and up the stairs to stay with a woman named Carmen in a green house on stilts.

Our group's mission in Gandoca was to help ensure the survival of the world's largest species of sea turtle, the leatherback, which grows to six or seven feet in length and weighs upward of fifteen hundred pounds. Unlike the shells of other sea turtles, the bony plates of the leatherback carapace rest under the animals' tough, oily skin, not overtop it. Their backs look like a landscape of blue-black peaks and valleys with five dorsal ridges running vertically down the length.

Our second orientation was held under the palm-leaf roof of the village pavilion. We learned via a projector slideshow that there were two main threats to the leatherbacks' survival: egg loss and pollution. Leatherback eggs are dug up and eaten by birds, mammals, crustaceans, and sometimes humans, though human poaching wasn't a concern given the community's involvement in the project. Normally, nest loss is just one part of the larger ecosystem—the birds have to eat something, after all—but fishing nets and trash were taking a toll on the adult population. Leatherbacks' main source of food is jellyfish, which bear more than a passing resemblance to floating plastic. Turtles gulp down plastic bags, which mangle their guts, and then, sometimes, they die. Population decline in adults necessitated our intervention at the earliest and most accessible stage of the turtle life cycle, the egg.

As volunteers, we were told, we would rotate through two jobs: beach patrols and hatchery duty. Maps and diagrams *ka-chunk-clicked* onto the projector screen, illustrating how the two established hatcheries were fenced off above ground, while below ground, wire mesh provided additional protection. During hatchery duty then, all we really had to do was sit in a lean-to and stare at the sand, watching for signs of hatching. Sharp-sighted volunteers might notice a growing depression in the ground, the myopic, a jumble of little green bodies climbing out of the earth. Those lucky volunteers staffing a shift when hatchlings emerged were to count, measure, and weigh them and then supervise their determined flop out to sea.

On beach patrol, which was broken into four-hour shifts covering all the dark hours, we would follow an experienced team leader along the shoreline, looking for nesting females. If a turtle was spotted, the leader would determine if the nest needed to be relocated, depending on factors like beach erosion and distance from the hatcheries—a clutch farther from the hatcheries was more likely to be relocated for easier supervision. If the eggs required relocation, the patrol team would wait quietly while this magnificent relic from the age of dinosaurs built her nest, laid her eggs, and crawled back into the ocean. Then the volunteers would carefully excavate the nest and pilfer her babies for safekeeping.

I was assured that in early summer, the likelihood that I would see a turtle nesting during one of my patrols on this beach was so high that it was almost a sure thing. Volunteers in the previous two weeks had seen up to twelve females laying each night. I had in fact watched such an event several times on television, but when Jeff Corwin stood next to a leatherback and expressed his rapid, hushed, musical admiration, the dimension of time was accelerated in ways I conveniently forgot; instead I was aware of the way the enormity of the experience, the dimensions of sheer physical size, had been reduced. The overall effect on the version of me sitting with rapt attention before the day-dimmed slides that afternoon was considerable. I expected to be marked indelibly by the experience. I believed that after such a sighting, my abstract sense of where meaning resided in my life (animals, helping them) would congeal into a solid thing, one I could carry with me like a stone, not a burden but a weight to ground me.

I say this in hindsight as a way of trying to make sense of what eventually happened to me on the trip, but to suggest that I was searching for something isn't quite right. In fact, I had never had reason to doubt much of anything in the grand scheme of things. Even if I didn't quite believe in God anymore, I still believed in an abiding goodness in the way events unfolded. I had every assurance that life would turn out well for me and no sense of how it might not. What I was about to discover was how fragile that sureness was, how little disappointment it took for me to abandon the macheted jungle path of my dreams and wander off into the existential bog. The truer setup is one in which I come to the beach already carrying the stone, only to realize that in my hands, it has all the weight and integrity of a plastic bag.

•••••••

During the first meal I ate in the green house on stilts, I sat with Karen and was mildly embarrassed to be served by Carmen. I have always been a guilt-ridden guest, once offering to reimburse my friend's parents for the water I used to take a shower, and my Spanish was mostly limited to *por favor*, *gracias*, and the numbers one through twenty-nine. These thirty-one words, I soon found, fell short of facilitating the kind of cultural immersion I'd been imagining. Later on in the trip, while I was ordering chicken and rice from a menu, my covolunteers would chide me with a good-heartedness I didn't deserve for pronouncing *pollo* with an *l*.

But that evening, I would go on my first patrol, and I was excited. We were not allowed to wear bug spray because the chemicals in the repellant could transfer to the eggs and damage them, so I covered my legs with khaki pants and, as a compromise given the heat and humidity, paired them with a T-shirt. I knew mosquitos would bite me, but that was a necessary discomfort with which I was already familiar. I slid my flashlight into my pocket, ensuring the red film filter I had rubber-banded on top was secure, as unfiltered white light was known to drive turtles back into the ocean.

I set off for Hatchery B and there met my patrol, led by Marta, a graduate student in biology. Our IST group was not the only set of volunteers in the village, and as I stumbled into the night, I got to know some of the others—from Germany, the Netherlands, Spain, and the US. I had a great time taking with Jordan, a self-described "post-God, ethnic Jew" who was headed to Columbia as a journalism grad student that fall. Our conversation was strange and slightly exhilarating because we seemed to be flirting, but in the pitch black of nonindustrialized night, neither of us could quite make out what the other person looked like.

The beach was not easy to walk along even in the daytime. The shoreline swept in and out from a line of palm trees, and in some stretches, a wide bed of sand gradually rose to the palms. In others, the point where the sand met the tree line was an abrupt vertical drop-off into the water. The waves were steadily eroding these sections, and fallen palm trees intermittently lay across our path along with huge logs that drifted onshore from distant lumber operations. Here, the waves crashed into you as you marched. When we waded across estuaries, I worried about rumors of crocodiles, but the more present problem was my wet boots. Once wet, they collected clumps of sand like concrete, which made walking effectively in the dark even more difficult. I soon realized that the red-filtered flashlight provided so little illumination it was not worth the hassle of carrying. Given my poor night vision, that first night I fell a lot and didn't see any turtles.

I arrived back at Carmen's house at four in the morning and tried to unstick as much sand from my body as possible before lying down on the bed behind my mosquito net. The patrol had been difficult—though I wouldn't realize the full extent of the sandfly attack until the next morning—but in the way I assumed all meaningful work and all adventures must be. I felt like I had passed a test.

• • • • • • •

In my downtime, I started to get to know the other students and volunteers better, despite complaining in my journal that this felt like a waste of my time. "I'm a biologist, not an anthropologist," I wrote, though I was neither. The Dutch and German men were all attractive and articulate in their equal disdain for American politics and American-sized tubs of peanut butter, and my fellow students were mostly nice, smart kids with quirks and backstories I can still recall twenty years later. Amy was learning to rock climb and most days could be found hanging from any horizontal structure that would support her weight, trying to do chin-ups. Jackie, who was tall, blond, and abrasive, was the only person I didn't like, but this is not a story about other people's failings; it is a story about mine.

Sometimes I had nighttime hatchery duty, and other than making a few periodic trips around the structure with another weak flashlight, there was nothing to do but sit in the dark next to a stranger and talk. Something about the blank expanse of those nights always led to secret hurts: three times, the person I was sitting next to spontaneously told me something terrible. One told me that her father had recently drunk himself to death, another that she had been raped, and another that she'd tried to end her own life multiple times. There was something of the middle school sleepover in these moments, the understanding that we were all steadily moving toward Truth instead of Dare and that when the time came, we wanted to be the one holding the most devastating revelation. I had no traumas or heartbreaks to share and could only reply that I was sorry. For pete's sake, I was still a virgin. When the sun broke through pink on the horizon, I thought *Dare* and headed out to check the nests.

•••••••

The mosquitos were starting to be a problem for me, and the sandflies were even worse. After Costa Rica, I started paying more attention to relative human suffering in bug-infested environments and found that I fare spectacularly poorly. The science behind *why* some people are more attractive to mosquitoes than others isn't conclusive, but we definitely know that some people *are*. Susceptibility is thought to be largely genetic, which correlates to what I've seen. If there are ten mosquitoes within a hundred square yards of my father and me, five are biting him, five are biting me, and everyone else is wondering what the hell my dad and I are complaining about. One summer—fourteen years after Costa Rica—I was working on an organic farm pulling weeds in wet dirt on an overcast day. It was the only day the whole summer the mosquitoes were out, and it was the only day all summer I did some loud complaining. No one else was being bitten, and the four other workers, all my superiors, seemed to think I was exaggerating my distress. When I got home, I counted thirty-eight welts on my left arm and scapula alone.

In conversations other volunteers translated for me, the locals in Costa Rica seemed to indicate they weren't especially bothered by the insects, and of the volunteers, no one looked as bad as I did. I looked very bad. Mosquito bites are usually flattish and white, but sandfly bites are hard, red, and raised. My legs were covered in them.

On the adventure half of the tour, men would walk by and point at my legs, laughing. *Mosquito* comes to English from Spanish, so for once I knew what they were saying. Four months passed before the more than two hundred purplish spots the bites left behind started to fade.

The bite problem was exacerbated by the fact that I couldn't ever get myself or my bed entirely clean. Our shower was a hose that ran down from a cistern that collected rainwater, and while the system was pretty good given the circumstances, it produced no water pressure. No matter how long I stood under the hose, I couldn't get all the sand off my body. Back in my bed, I would lie down in my gritty sheets and try to fall asleep. The sand would rub against my fly bites, and I'd get more and more claustrophobic with every breath. The sensation didn't hurt so much as it drove me slowly insane.

If my admission that a large part of my torment in Costa Rica was due to itchiness strikes you as pathetic, I agree. But consider, too, that our intolerances differ. I've traveled to and lived in other climates in the time since my turtle expedition, and I've now got a good sense of what does and doesn't bother me. In my journal, I speculated that I was better suited for the high desert or the Pacific Northwest—one of the few imaginings I entertained that month that turned out to be true. I can do cold. I can do arid. I can do rain. I do well at altitude, and I'm built for carrying heavy loads on my back. What I'm not made for is humid heat—I wither pathetically and can't think straight—and I have absolutely no resilience against itchiness.

In terms of strength and cardiovascular endurance, I was in the best shape of my life. I'd just completed a season of collegiate rowing, and rowing is nothing if not an exercise in managing physical strain. But the Costa Rican shoreline jungle exploited all of my bodily weaknesses: it was hot, humid, sandy, and buggy. The environment wore on me physically and psychologically, and I was deeply disappointed by my lack of fortitude in the face of these simple creature discomforts.

So there was that weakness of the body, which I dragged along with my hope as I continued to go out on patrols and see little more than the shadow of the back of the person in front of me. The only animal I had seen at night emerged from the tree line, a pair of eyes that came up to my chest. The form materialized into the pony-sized wolfhound that ran loose around the village. I started to worry that I would never see a turtle, and I began to suspect that sometimes, suffering came without reward.

While I grew intimate with the soul-crushing boredom of waiting for the natural world to do something worthy of television, the leatherbacks, never having seen a wildlife documentary, continually missed their cue.

•••••••

I was also homesick and lonely. By the end of the month-long trip, I was a well-liked and integral member of the group, still able to set a mini-bus full of young people chuckling, but at the beach, I mostly listened and then complained in my journal. After just five days, I wrote: "I'm experiencing some sort of malaise. I'm not enjoying much, which is a sore disappointment. Do I really want to travel? Do I want to do research? Do I actually care about anything anymore?" It's shocking how quickly I got there, though I commanded myself to stop feeling that way, though I kept returning to the leatherbacks as the solution, convinced that when I finally saw a turtle nesting, it would all suddenly make sense.

"I just want to see some goddamn sea turtles," I pouted.

Right around the time that I admitted to myself I was miserable, my group hiked to a permaculture farm a few miles down the shore. The farm was mostly run by a group of white American immigrants. By the end of the tour, I had learned how the inhabitants utilized their solid waste to generate methane to heat their water and that most of the residents' time was spent growing marijuana and meditating in the yoga temple. They served us a meal, and the greens tasted like the maple leaves I once chewed on out of curiosity as a kid. All the residents were beautiful, and half of them were half naked.

I wonder now if some part of the frustration that finally undid me in Gandoca wasn't sexual. I spent at least as much time writing about my attraction to Jörn, a volunteer from Hamburg, and speculating about whether the fit young woman who helped me lug my kayak to the lagoon had a crush on me—she danced the male part of the salsa when music played in the pavilion and gave my head a pat/squeeze that seemed flirtatious—as I did chronicling the anguished state of my big turtle lust. I wasn't just a virgin. I hadn't even kissed anyone.

• • • • • • •

Finally, there were hatchlings. When the first little one pulled itself free from the sand, Karen and I filled the large plastic tub in the shack with cool, moist sand and started plucking the flopping miniatures up from their sprint to the ocean and placing them in the tub. I located the black case containing the equipment we were to use for data collection. We had been instructed not to touch the hatchlings with our bare hands. Inside the case, I found a single latex glove with four fingers intact, and in the back of the shed, we located some deteriorating, rained-on papers attached to a clipboard—the instruction manual on how to proceed.

I knew we were supposed to take a count, weigh and measure a certain number of the hatchlings, and record ground temperatures in a few different places around the nest.

"Are we supposed to measure the length to the end of the tail?" I asked.

Karen was flipping through the papers. She held up a hand-drawn diagram that looked like a wobbly circle with a triangle on the top and bottom. A bracket encompassed the entire drawing, and the words "measure like this" were written beside it.

Karen held a ruler in the general vicinity of a flailing turtle and made an estimate. We then searched for the scale, which turned out to be the bottom half of a twenty-ounce plastic Coke bottle paper-clipped to a hanging scale. I picked up the baby turtle whose length we'd just guessed and held it in my four gloved fingers, pulling my bare index finger as far back as I could. Even if the turtle would have fit in the pop-bottle basket, which it didn't, it was, as it had been programmed by evolution to do, thrashing its flippers violently, trying to launch itself forward off anything it could. The bigger turtles simply wouldn't fit, which would skew the data miserably, and I didn't want to risk any of them falling out of our ludicrous measuring tool.

I said fuck it.

I retrieved the digital thermometer, the one piece of equipment that looked up to par, carried it outside the shack like an altar boy bearing gifts, and placed it into the sand. I watched as the numbers appeared on the read-out screen. I read them aloud to Karen as they climbed: forty-eight, sixty-one, seventy-five, seventy-seven. Then the numbers became erratic, making huge jumps up and down every few seconds.

In seventh-grade math class, I once got a detention because I couldn't shut up about what I considered the impossibility of accurate measurement. "If we can divide an inch into smaller and smaller units, how we can we *ever settle* on how big something is?" On the beach that day, kneeling before a machine, I would have settled for even a ten-degree error.

This is research? I thought. *These are the tools of experts?* Though I now know that most fieldwork is better organized and most data more fastidiously monitored, in the lean-to I stared down an eruption of wriggling, chaotic life, and instead of feeling joy, I was quietly crushed by human imprecision. Back in school that fall, while I completed one more quarter as a biology major and earned the highest score out of three hundred some students on my first few organic chemistry exams, I glared suspiciously at my TAs when they misspelled bases and even developed a paranoia about global warming science. Lucky for me, my friend Kelsey studied with Lonnie Thompson, the world's foremost authority on ice cores, and whenever I started to worry aloud that someone had made a dire miscalculation, she'd patiently explain it to me all over again. Once while visiting for Christmas, she drew me a graph plotting CO_2 concentrations and global temperatures over time with her gloved hand in the snow.

In the turtle hut, we counted the hatchlings, held the ruler up to a few more, and then tipped the tub over. I had heard this moment described by other people with a sort of lyricism—watching the newly hatched young charge instinctively into the depths, leaving the safety of the nest to disappear into a world of great peril. We were not allowed to aid them, as real biologists hypothesized the female turtles' trek into the water was necessary if they were to find their way back out of it onto this beach someday. I wondered about finding my own way back home.

•••••••

I was sulking, and everyone else in my group seemed to be having a good time. The other volunteers had either seen a turtle nesting or liked the beach or were just better at creating meaningful diversions for themselves while on fruitless beach patrols and in the long stretches of downtime. My body was wrecked, and I seemed incapable of appreciating anything that wasn't a fifteen-hundred-pound reptile lumbering up the shore to impart some great secret to me, her audience, whom the turtle didn't consider merely inconsequential but, of course, didn't consider at all.

I went on my final beach patrol, and that night, I fell asleep while sitting on a log and tumbled face-first into the sand. By this time, I had suffered my great disappointment. Instead of laughing, as I had done after my fall in the Miami hotel room, I barely kept myself from crying.

•••••••

On our last night in Gandoca, in the pavilion in front of the shop that sold shelf-safe milk and candy bars that had the particular taste and texture of having melted and recongealed, my group met to discuss what we had learned during our two-week stay and what changes we anticipated making once we got home.

My fellow volunteers made a lot of self-righteous proclamations about bananas (boycotting them to bring about more humane working conditions on the plantations) and bicycles (how everyone should always ride one, since surely every place had weather as nice as Santa Barbara). I tried to amuse myself by coming up with a series of warnings for the sort of wildlife show I felt had led me astray:

> Warning: The events in this program are a reconstruction. In order to provide the twenty-two minutes of wildlife footage you are about to see, the camera crew and intrepid biologist-host had to endure at least three weeks of torture. Do not under any circumstances expect an expedition into

the wild to result in fun, enlightenment, or contact with creatures other than parasites.

Warning: Content has been edited. Conscientious parents should supply correctives to these fantasies in the form of reality-based play with children, such as rubbing them with poison ivy, dumping sand in their underwear, and poking them with needles.

Frankly, I felt unstable.

Someone was trying to make a point about conserving water by turning the shower off while you lathered, and someone else was talking over him about how much she had learned about cooperation. The woman who lived in the house in front of the pavilion was chasing her toddler and hitting her with a hairbrush. I was swatting mosquitos and scratching my itchy legs.

And then I snapped.

I remember feeling a strange, expanding sensation while also thinking the world had opened up to swallow me. I moaned. Out loud.

"Oh my god, you guys," I said. "You guys, what's the point?"

People turned to look at me.

I'm not sure what they saw, but there I was—a sad and confused young woman far away from home, sitting in a plastic lawn chair facing the end of meaning.

"I mean. Just like. What's the point?"

Jackie didn't miss a beat. "Take a fucking ecology class!" she hissed. "Then you'll know the point!" She began detailing the ecological intricacies of a planet that now seemed at once strange and trivial to me: "If the turtles die, then the jellyfish and sponges become overpopulated, and then the zooplankton die, and then the whole fucking food chain is destroyed! *That's* the fucking point!"

I don't remember what I said in response or if I said anything at all. I do know that later that night there was music, and in the knowledge that I had two more weeks here among these people who were not yet my friends in this place that was not my home, I moved my body in time with the music in the semblance of someone dancing. Later, on the adventure tour, I was stung by a scorpion and then a jellyfish. I was equal parts unfit and unlucky.

•••••••

My friend Kelsey, my advisor on global warming, is hardcore. She's a herpetologist who's spent years in Costa Rica and Peru studying peccary shit and glacial frogs, and her fieldwork is always rife with misery. In the Costa Rican rain forest, she conducts her work among sharp bamboo stalks, wearing thick pants and long-sleeve shirts in extreme heat. She ties a bandana across the bottom half of her face so she doesn't aspirate swarming bugs. In the Andean mountains, she packs in to her work site everything she and her field assistant need for two weeks at a time. She sleeps in a tent at seventeen thousand feet. She shits in the open air next to glaciers.

Her tolerance for hardship mirrors her capacity for joy. She claims to not be a morning person, but the last time I visited her, she rose from a floor mat ten mornings in a row, bouncing up and down while reciting the meals we would eat that day. When she recently tried and failed to scale a volcano, she cursed the mountain, not herself.

My failure in Costa Rica was manifold. I went on the trip to help save the world's largest sea turtle, and I never saw one. I felt devastated but was also unable to view my sorrow as legitimate. Neither, however, could I make it go away.

What I'd gone looking for in Costa Rica was a spectacle, and what I'd found was a series of profound mismatches. The fulfillment and enjoyment I expected to derive from work I thought meaningful and the muted reality. The scope of the world and the insignificance of my little desires. What I saw instead of a turtle was what a paltry thing my wonder was and how capacious my instinct for disappointment. Likely, I would have stood a few feet from the largest sea turtle on earth and thought, *So that's a turtle,* and gone right back to lamenting my physical circumstances.

I went to Costa Rica, and my charmed life cracked a little, exposing my ridiculous expectations and my silly, heavy sadness. Two thousand miles from home, I sat beside strangers in a hut until, for the first time, the universe itself became unfamiliar. Then, even stranger yet, I stumbled across myself.

I came home from Costa Rica and sat on the couch, stupefied. I announced to my parents that I was no longer sure what to do with myself. I gave up my rowing training regimen and a few months into school again changed my major to literature. That next summer, I lived with my sister in Cincinnati and worked in the corporate picnicking area of an amusement park, disseminating hot dogs and potato salad, hauling garbage bags of uneaten baked beans out to the dumpster at twilight. I read a lot of books, and in one of them Erich Fromm mused that the material components of the human body were worth about ninety-eight cents. When I read that, I fell again, this time rolling on the carpet of my sister's apartment, screaming with laughter. Sometimes at the amusement park, when my arms were submerged among soapy clumps of macaroni noodles at the dish station, or when the baked beans split the garbage bags open and cascaded to the floor in a viscous waterfall, I felt peaceful—far indeed from asking the cosmos to deliver me something grand that I might fail to appreciate.

WITH MEN

THE TROUBLE WITH LOVING POETS

The trouble with loving poets is that they leave a long paper trail. They want you to read it too. So back you go, stepping lightly, trying not to stumble over fragments of old lovers lying about in line after line. Thighs there, a mouth there, and wow, whose tits are those? They sure don't look like yours.

A lot of musicians are just poets who carry guitars, because guitars are like special shields that protect you from violence when you want to speak poetically in public. I once dated a man named David who walked around with a guitar slung over his shoulder like a submachine gun. He was always pointing it at me and breaking into songs about his old girlfriends. I'd blush and not know where to put my eyes, the guitar on his lap between us having grown obscene.

Tottering about his house, I was like an uncouth child in a museum of the heart's artifacts: pottery, paintings, embroidered pillows. In everything he owned lingered the traces of other women. Sometimes I got hungry and wanted Cheerios.

"Not that bowl!" David would cry, snatching the dish out of my hands and clutching it to his chest. "It's from Almina, and she's very, very special."

I was wary of the ghosts who haunted that house, who floated around in my brain with their delicate bones and uncanny talents: girls with genius grants, polyglots with nuanced accents, virgins, he said, with vaginas like nasal passages.

Probably that blue-black bowl would've slipped right out of my hands. In those days, I was clumsy with love.

HUNG UP

I

I didn't set out to find a big penis. In the years before I met Kevin, I had no reason to be unsatisfied. I'd been in several long-term relationships, and in every one, I adored my partner's cock. I loved it, admired it, desired it, and never felt it could be improved in any way. But with Kevin, I was obsessed.

Kevin was possessed of an exquisitely proportioned eight-inch penis. It was the first thing I thought about when I woke up in the morning and the object of dazed longing throughout the day. Dubious science tells us that women aren't wired for visual stimulation, but let me tell you: I loved looking. Kevin's dick was very straight. He was circumcised. His testicles hung loose and low. He wasn't theatrical and never indicated that his penis was something to be worshipped or reckoned with or even prioritized.

He was, in fact, a quiet man. Shy, introverted. His inwardness made the towering exteriority of his arousal that much more thrilling. *Speak softly,* T.R. said. You know the rest.

Because Kevin himself stood tall and thin, the scale of his sex alongside his thighs was stunning. Our own sex was effortless and anti-gymnastic—whatever the angle, he could cover the distance. The *reach* of that thing. Eventually I realized he was seeing other women, and then his reach came to seem inescapable. I tried and failed to stop seeing him over and over, even moving two hours north after I discovered that at a distance of less than fifty miles, I automatically contacted him.

In the end, the struggle was taken out of my hands. Kevin started exclusively dating someone who was not me, and I was left all hung up on a hung man.

II

After months of despondency, I started to date again. I went on a few dates with men I wasn't especially attracted to, and then I met Joe. In most ways, Joe was exactly my type: goofy, gifted, barely fiscally solvent. He was a musician in his late thirties who worked in a pizza shop and authored a newsletter called *Pie Times*. On our first date, our conversation made clear that we had scrutinized and approved of each other's responses to the dating site's sex questions. On paper, we were a great match, the data suggesting—he quipped—that we should have sex right away and continuously. So when I decided not to go home with him that night, I think I surprised both of us. I simply wasn't ready for the big reveal.

I talked at length about my predicament with friends, while in private I told myself I was being ridiculous. My admission of having desperately fallen for a great big penis was in the least impolite, flying in the face of standard "size doesn't matter" affirmations I personally felt were important.

But I also knew that I was fundamentally wrong: size *doesn't* matter. All the reassurances offered to straight men with shorter-than-average penises are true. For most women, girth and stiffness are more intimately tied to pleasure than length, and penetration isn't how we're going to come anyway. For most women, the hundreds of other things that make a person a good mate are more important than penis size. After my time with Kevin, though, my expectations had exponentially grown, and only along one dimension.

I was surprised to find myself in this position, as I had spent many former years maniacally investigating how *I* compared to the previous lovers of previous lovers. How large were her breasts? Could she have G-spot orgasms? How did she feel about anal sex? As with many things I felt insecure about, I thought laying out and confronting all the facts of my partners' sexual histories, even those in which I stacked up poorly (I can orgasm only with clitoral stimulation; I'll pass on anal), was preferable to living with my runaway imaginings.

Tall with broad shoulders, I sometimes wondered which anatomical tier I belonged to in an ancient, animal-themed taxonomy for sexual compatibility I'd once heard my parents laugh about: Was I an "elephant woman" who could match only with an elephant man? But when I asked Kevin about my own comparative size, he first made a circle with his thumb and index finger and then ran his finger down his thumb, shrinking the diameter. He asked, "This way?"

"Yeah."

And he said, "It's on the smaller side."

In solving certain problems, Kevin opened others. Now suddenly I was worried my next partner would disappoint *me*. The worry behind all of my concerns was the same, however: the worry that somewhere, somehow, someone was having better sex than I was. And the source of this anxiety, I knew, was my parents.

Yes, my parents and all their well-intentioned, Masters-and-Johnson openness. "Sex is a gift," we were told, and our mother was particularly gifted. My dad once told us kids, "Your mother is a sex goddess," and where he saw himself exercising sex positivity, I saw a benchmark.

With Kevin, sex was better than I had ever thought possible, so much love it broke the scale. My great pleasure was due in part to his skill, in part to his personality and presentation. But mostly, I thought, it was due to his large part.

III

When I finally did go home with Joe, both the first and the second time, the sex went badly. But our foundering had little to do with Joe's penis size, which was—just as his name portended—perfectly average. We were incredibly attracted to each other, but under the long shadow of our exes, we couldn't seem to make it work.

The second night I stayed over, after our second disappointment, I mentioned to him that I thought my head was too small for my body. I had nothing to worry about, he said, and besides, his situation was worse: his head was too large. He then listed and extolled all of the small-headed people and dogs in his life.

As we were falling asleep, I remember Joe saying something to himself very slowly, taking pleasure in each syllable as he recalled a word, while I lay quiet and felt my heart grow two sizes. *Mi-cro-ce-pha-ly*, he whispered.

Reader, we persevered.

Back to the foot of the peak we went, and together we climbed—up, up, up, up—until finally, down into the quaking valley we plummeted, one at a time. We laughed. We high-fived. And from that old, comfortable place, the fear of disappointment started to inch away.

I was shocked to find that the grand lasciviousness I had felt with Kevin was not a peculiarity. Even more than I had wanted Kevin's penis, now I wanted Joe's, and not in spite of its standard size: I wanted *that* one, exactly as it was, lovely and violet-tinged. At times, I wondered aloud if I had stumbled into a male fantasy, given how going down on Joe left my thighs drenched. But I also liked my own body so much that such anticipation—*Like spring water!* Joe himself gushed—accompanied the simple act of dressing myself to see him.

Perhaps, I started to think, this pleasure wasn't centered in any specific organ at all. Perhaps, I thought, *just perhaps,* this pleasure was centered in me.

IIII

Not long after I met Joe, I was offered a job out of state, and we parted ways. In a new town, I soon met other men and pursued my suspicions, testing my desire, observing it, steeping in it. I sat on a couch alongside a reserved man who later said that as a principle, he had never had sex on a first date. But the evening we met, he reached to put his arm around me and we just kept sliding, melting into an insistent heat until his principle was shed like so much clothing. His penis was marvelous, big with a pronounced downward bend I loved to unfurl.

At an outdoor bar table, I sat across from another man who was not at all reserved and a good deal shorter than I was, and I listened while he spoke as directly as I was wont to about things

I had often wondered. He rattled off a set of rhetorical questions about the anxiety of measuring up: Who knows how we compare? Are you really tall? Am I really short? Are we going to sleep together tonight, and is what I'm working with enough? Questions answered, joyfully, in little time. His penis curved upward and pressed like a grip, a sensation that was not only enough but entirely new and exhilarating.

These scenes and others played over and over in my head while I walked about the world, throbbing. I was back in a daze, and this time with equal billing. My desire had its own generous reach, a two-pronged thing that wanted both men and myself. In place of a fantasy life crowded with comparisons and anxieties, I dwelled in the gift my body was in the company of another—a long form of curves and mounds, a center that kicked and carried its own pulse.

•••••••

On one of my many failed attempts to get away from Kevin, I took a trip to Iceland. I'd heard Reykjavík boasted the world's only phallological museum, and I couldn't resist. I soon found myself staring at a taxidermized elephant dong protruding several feet from its mount on the wall. A full range of mammalian members was on display, from the prodigious to the miniscule, as well as some dicks of dubious origin (merman, troll). The complete tour took only a few minutes, and soon I was in the gift shop buying an "It's All About Dicks" tote bag and thinking, in predictable fashion, that the museum was much smaller than I had expected. And besides, I'd seen an elephant dick before.

My sister and I were on safari at Kruger National Park, sitting in a tiny sports car driven by our Afrikaner guide. Blocking the road ahead was an enormous bull elephant. The elephant was in musth, the telltale secretions showing wet on the skin below its temples, and there, like a slick fifth leg, hung its engorged dick. The previous day, I'd had several uncomfortable interactions with the guide, who insisted on hugging me and then conversing with me about my physical features—my face, my height. Frowning at him and withering into myself did nothing to deter him. Now, he drove slowly toward the elephant and thought of a game. He zoomed a little past the bull and then threw the car into reverse, backing up until we were facing it again. He repeated this maneuver, back and forth, back and forth, taunting the elephant in a car it could easily crush. Finally he cried, "They say the lion's the king of the jungle, but what do you think of *that*?"

•••••••

The world still does not know what to make of a woman's wanting. We demand it where it does not exist, her tepid responses leading to frightening provocations. A grown man goaded me with a six-foot animal dick. Or we turn away from it, as if in a world where "no mean yes," the message "yes, yes, yes, yes, now" is nothing short of a turnoff.

If the old story says female desire is most attractive when left unspoken, or when obliquely implied, then let me make things difficult by saying it plainly. I am not a metaphorical elephant woman in need of a metaphorical elephant penis. But once, not so long ago, I fell for a great big one I thought would be the end of pleasure. But I kept looking, and with time, I found something even more profound: a great, big, deep knowing. The only size that ever mattered was the size of my wanting. And my want, like that of many, many women, was gigantic.

DUMPED

Over the course of about thirteen years, until I had the good sense to give up, I was dumped by roughly ten men. During that time, I ended exactly one relationship; also once, I decided in agreement with another person that we should no longer date each other.

None of my breakups with these men were what I would call "bad." Painful, yes, confusing, sure. Always, I reacted to them with a mix of sadness and obsessive reckoning. I have written and spoken hundreds of thousands of words with the intention of either reasoning someone back into my life or convincing them they have made a logical error in failing to recognize my value. All of the men I put through these exit interviews were exceedingly patient. Not one regretted breaking up with me.

Despite my exhaustive attention to detail in each, the dialogues tended to be iterative. Shortly after having "one last talk," I was again seized with the conviction that my lingering unease could be remedied by one *more* last talk. What I wanted most was a good goodbye, a joint resolution that left no stone unturned, until—there! finally!—my dignity was revealed.

My last great appeal was made to a man who cited his ill mother, his DUI, and his "not being in the right place" as reasons we should end our relationship. I had already explained compellingly how I could be a *solution* to all of these problems, but he was not convinced. I saw that we were through. As always, though, untidy feelings and thoughts swirled around me, and I believed if we could talk just one more time, I could finally move on. I emailed him my request from home while I sat eating a piece of red velvet cake procured from a fast-food restaurant. In an ad that told me, "Dinner isn't over until you've had dessert," the complimentary cake was touted as "the big finish" to a ten-piece meal I'd shared with my family. I chewed on my finale until I saw he had agreed to meet.

The next day, we reconvened in his dimly lit living room and started to talk, but he seemed distracted by the clock, wanting to be sure he was ready to go when his ride elsewhere arrived. I had a time limit. I sat across from him and with dexterity started gathering all of my strands—my grievances, my questions, my hurts, my hopes—pulling them out and up and together over the top of the large, awkward box containing my feelings about our relationship. I reached out to tie the bow, which now, I thought, would be both neat and little.

But before I could quite accomplish this feat of self-preservation, the urgency of the time limit was suddenly replaced by a much greater urgency to empty my bowels. *The cake*, I thought. *That grotesquely red cake.*

I have a stalwart digestive system, but over the course of several softball seasons in my teens, I seem to have sensitized it to red food coloring through the superstitious consumption of an obscene quantity of Twizzlers. At the start of every weekend tournament, I would eat an entire package of family-size Twizzlers by myself in the car on the way. This, at any rate, is my theory for why on rare but acute occasions after eating something stained with red dye, the workings of my intestines present themselves to me in lamentation.

I stopped dead in my tracks as I felt certain pressures shift.

"Wow, I . . . I am feeling sick. I'm, um. I'm going to go to the bathroom, and it might be a while."

"Okay," he said, in a neutral tone.

I rose to a hunched position, measuring his face for concern.

The bathroom was down the hall past a spare bedroom so stuffed full of junk that I had never been allowed to enter. I managed once again to wonder about its contents as I scooted by. I made it to the bathroom, sat on the toilet, and closed the flimsy door. Now my attention narrowed. *Oh my god.*

I could feel the sludge inside of me pressing down hard, ready to fill the vacuous quiet of the bathroom in its plummet, but I was still desperately hoping to attenuate the flow rate. It was the auditory horror I feared most. That he would *hear* my gastric undoing. I willed my sphincters to let me down gently.

And then in a torrent it came, a watery expulsion I could not control, in unceasing rounds. I pressed my hands against the walls on either side of me and raised my feet onto tiptoes. I bared my teeth. My disgrace continued to discharge itself into the toilet.

Eventually the span of time in between bouts lengthened, and the duration of the bouts themselves shortened. I waited until I was sure the fusillade was over, and then I cleaned myself up, washed my hands, and set out to face a considerably altered rhetorical situation.

"I'm so sorry. I never get sick. I have a very stalwart digestive system."

"Are you all right?"

"Yeah, I think so. Oh my god, could you hear me? I just had explosive diarrhea."

"Oh, not really. I thought you were throwing up."

We looked at each other.

"Well, my ride is going to be here any minute."

"Yeah, right, okay. I guess I'll head out then. Wow, this really didn't turn out like I planned."

We laughed a little, he deigned to hug me, and I left in a fluster. "Okay, take care," I blabbered on my way out the door, "bye."

• • • • • • •

After my crucifixion on the toilet, my grip came loose. I gave up my post-breakup explications and then, in my finest release, quit dating altogether.

With the new time I found after abandoning companionship work, I put my restorative impulses to better use and remodeled a house. One of the first projects I undertook was adding an overhead vent to the bathroom where there had been none. I was discussing the installation with an electrician, who advised me to pick up the box and consider the sones printed on the label: "That's the measure of how much noise it makes. You're going to want a fan with a sone level below one and a half."

I glanced at the box sitting on the other side of the room but did not get up. "Yes, I know what sones are. I picked the loudest fan I could find."

When I switch on the vent in my own bathroom, I don't intend to muffle the warning still thundering forward from that day years past, but now, at least, my guests can be spared my epiphany. In my house, the fan roars steadily but without bitterness, in decency, not denial, placed with an equanimity of mind I know could never have been but for the brutal lesson of my body, its rupturing of sense and control. *Who are you kidding?* my guts said. *Closure?*

Absent my plunge on the toilet, I'd never have spotted the ugly truth lurking behind my interrogations and flowcharts and exasperating need for a tidy separation, which is that there are no good goodbyes when you're hurting, only the *but, but, but* sputtering of asses and mouths.

WITH US

HPV AND THE BURDEN OF KNOWLEDGE

All I wanted for my thirtieth birthday was an HPV test. The previous year, at age twenty-nine, I'd asked my provider to run the screening in addition to a standard STI panel at my annual women's health exam, but she declined. "All your recent paps have been normal. There's no need for an HPV test."

I'd had one abnormal but ambiguous pap result in the past but never an HPV test, and by twenty-nine, I knew enough about HPV to realize that a normal pap result didn't necessarily mean you didn't have HPV—it just meant that your cervical cells weren't visibly mutated. I thought requesting a screening was the responsible thing to do, both for my own sake and potentially others', as I had been in an on-again, off-again relationship I wrongly assumed was monogamous when the switch was in the "on" position. "I'd like to be sure," I said, but my practitioner, a slight, middle-aged white woman with white hair, looked at me, shook her head mildly, and said something I never expected to hear from a doctor: "We'd rather not know."

I let the issue drop, content to follow protocol, but I was still puzzled by my doctor's response—her lab-coated shrug, the advice that we collectively look away. I tended to think of medicine as a discipline rather like myself, dedicated to the proposition that above all, we must strive for knowledge, particularly when that knowledge is difficult to hear.

When finally, at the age of thirty, I qualified for an elective screening, I was more than delighted to receive good news: negative. My relief was so palpable, I announced the results to a room full of women.

• • • • • • •

I don't recall learning about human papillomavirus until I went to college. In high school sex ed, HPV slid below my notice, overshadowed by HSV and HIV. In college, the information came via my housemate, who returned from a biology lecture and said her professor had issued a dire if somewhat tangential warning to the class about the increasing prevalence of HPV and its link to assorted cancers. The PSA had been complete with charts and flashy graphics.

At this point in my life, I'd had exactly one sexual partner, who'd similarly had exactly one sexual partner—me—so I wasn't worried. I took the lecture's message to heart, however, and concluded we were in the midst of a burgeoning public health crisis. I was already careful, but I resolved to be even more so. The new acronym lodged in the back of my mind, where it lay dormant.

Shortly after college, the three letters resurfaced during a confusing phone conversation with a nurse. She'd called with my pap results, and she seemed to be saying that everything was clear, that everything had resolved from my previous test.

"What?" I asked. "What previous test? My last test was normal."

"No, it looks like your last test had some borderline abnormal cells, but the doctor decided they were not of concern, so no further testing was ordered."

This was news to me.

"What does that mean exactly?"

"Well, it might indicate you had an HPV infection in the past, but it had already cleared."

Now a different triumvirate of letters popped into my head: *WTF? Why am I just hearing about this now?*

When I got off the phone, I talked the revelation over with my second sexual partner, who'd had several partners before me. We weren't sure what to do with the information. It sounded like we were in the clear, but perhaps for a time, in the past, we had not been. I was perplexed about why I had not been told.

Two years later, as a twenty-six-year-old graduate student, I sat on a crinkly examining table and did some quick math. I had just been offered the choice of getting a new vaccine for HPV, but I was told the injections were not covered by my student health insurance. The vaccine would be administered in multiple rounds totaling $1,000. As a teaching assistant, I made $13,000 a year, so the price tag was roughly 7 percent of my income. Aside from the confusing phone call about an HPV infection I may or may not have had at age twenty-four, I had no history of STIs. The man I was dating now had been a virgin when we met, and I was in love, sure we were going to be together forever.

"No," I decided. "I can't afford it. And I'm probably going to marry my boyfriend."

"Okay," my doctor said. "Just give us a call if you change your mind."

Two years after that, when my boyfriend broke up with me, I was beyond the age threshold for the vaccine.

• • • • • • •

I was out of school when my bad news came, and briefly, for a few hours, I lost my mind. Negative at thirty, positive at thirty-one. The nurse had put the news mildly, as she likely did to two or three women every week. *Abnormal pap with positive HPV. Come in for a colposcopy so we can take a closer look and a biopsy.*

I was still seeing the man whose lack of clarity on monogamy had first caused me to inquire about a screening, so I was confident I knew who had given me HPV and how. This certainty narrowed the beam of my frustration, but its target was on the other side of the country not answering his phone—in Portland, Oregon, in fact, visiting an artist friend I assumed he was also sleeping with. I had gathered the rough outline of this young woman's life via social media and conversations with the man I now believed had given me HPV.

When I finally got him on the phone, I shouted at him. He was never loquacious and was now completely silent. I don't know what I expected from him, and he did not apologize. Into the silence, I continued to pour my indignation: "Are you planning to tell the person you're out there sleeping with right now?"

He indicated he did not plan to mention my test results to his friend.

Probably what I should have done next was call my mother and cry. Instead, I sent a private message, an "HPV FYI," to the other woman. She replied shortly after to let me know the information had been received, and her words were so gentle, I was instantly stricken with remorse.

Though I had claimed the health of the young artist was foremost in my mind, I knew this was not true—I had acted in spite. Somewhere deep in a digital archive, the particulars of this exchange are buried, but I cannot bring myself to reexamine them.

The sentiments, though, are impossible to forget—my hysterical intrusion, her gracious reply.

In the years leading up to this day, medical protocol on HPV had denied me a phone call, a vaccine, and a test, leaving me instead with a void of information and a lack of control. On the day itself, a man with whom I'd been intimate for years offered me silence, while a woman whose own day I had intended to destroy offered me a simple acknowledgment that, comparatively, felt like a gesture of support.

• • • • • • •

After that, HPV seemed to explode in national discourse. Everywhere I looked, women were talking about HPV. On Twitter, Ayelet Waldman, taking a jab at Michele Bachmann and advocating for the Gardasil vaccine, disclosed that her husband, Pulitzer Prize–winning novelist Michael Chabon, had given her HPV. In *The New Yorker*, a friend of mine published a humor piece with HPV punchlines, jokes I was surprised to find were funnier now that I had HPV myself.

In film and stand-up, I watched as more women performed liberating excoriations. In *Obvious Child*, Jenny Slate's character leaves a series of deranged messages to her recent ex about his new partner, slurring, "Kate has . . . the kind of HPV where you get warts on your stuff and . . . ovarian cancer?" But the crown jewel of these commentaries was in *Baby Cobra,* Ali Wong standing on stage, pregnant in a loud print. After explaining that "HPV is a ghost that lives inside men's bodies and says, 'Boo' in women's," she taunts the crowd, claiming anyone who doesn't have HPV yet is "a fucking loser."

I posted the line about HPV saying "Boo" in women's bodies on Facebook, and in a sublime instant, my aunt tagged her husband in the comments. In public, then, I was hinting at outing myself. I assumed when the crucial moment came, I would be as brave as Ali Wong.

Of course, in *Obvious Child,* Slate's drunken rundown of HPV strains bungles a few key points. In claiming that Kate has "*the* kind of HPV" where you get both warts on your junk and cervical (not ovarian) cancer, she conflates low-risk (warts) and high-risk (cancer) HPV, though a given individual can have not only both types but also multiple strains of both types, all of which you can carry for decades without symptoms. *You,* in fact, probably *have* carried HPV: 80 percent of sexually active adults will have some form of HPV at some point in their lives.

I had an invisible, high-risk strain only, so I returned for a colposcopy and cervical biopsy. The biopsy was uncomfortable—three sharp pinches of tissue removed from an internal organ—and I was shocked by the quantity of blood left behind when I stood up. The results showed low-grade changes, so my new doctor, a woman who spoke English, Russian, Arabic, and French fluently and whom I found eminently admirable, told me the recommendation was to simply continue monitoring my cervix. In six months, I would need to return for another colposcopy. If after two years the infection had not resolved itself—in the vast majority of cases, the body clears the infection on its own, she said—only then would we proceed to a LEEP, the electrical excision of suspicious tissue. I knew what a LEEP was, had several friends who'd had the procedure, and was prepared for that course of action right away. What I was not prepared for was a strategy of wait and see.

Biding my time for six months while a "probably still positive" high-risk HPV diagnosis lurked in my cervix, receding, remaining static, or progressing, was not a treatment plan I had anticipated. I was starting to date again, hoping to finally disentangle myself from the unhealthy relationship I saw as the chief reason for my being in this doctor's office talking about cervical cancer in the first place. Now, evidently, the HPV was going to be carried forward into my reboot.

This persistence led to a new consideration. "Is this something I need to tell new partners about?" I asked.

I looked up at my doctor and waited for her answer as if from God. I wanted her to tell me exactly how to behave, to make the decision for me.

She shrugged. "It's really up to you. It's so common, as long as women are coming in for regular paps like they should, the risk is very low."

This, once again, was not the answer I had expected.

•••••••

I failed to disclose the fact that I had high-risk HPV to the first man I had sex with after my diagnosis. We were not new partners, but clearly, my status had changed since the last time we had been together several years earlier. I'd never had anything to disclose in the past nor, to my knowledge, had any of my partners, and my imagination and courage lacked the sharpness and strength to carve out the new space. As a famously forthright person, not to mention the daughter of sexually progressive and overeffusive parents, I could not fathom my timidity.

Rationalizations were easy to come by. First, my doctor hadn't expressly told me that I was obligated to disclose, and I knew that several friends who had HPV did not share this information with all their partners. Second, almost everyone had HPV at some point in their lives, and both types usually just went away—the likelihood of harm to straight, cis men in particular was incredibly low. Third, I used condoms, though I knew they were only somewhat effective in preventing transmission, as HPV lives in skin tissues. But the most compelling rationalization, the one I fell back on after first flogging myself for my cowardice, was the following: *There is no test for men.*

This, I felt, was the crux of the issue: my disclosure of high-risk HPV could never be reciprocated. When it comes to heterosexual PIV HPV, the knowledge that one is presently carrying a detectable, cancer-causing strain is a double-edged sword granted only to women. The risk of penile cancer from HPV is so low, the medical community has not developed a diagnostic test for it and does not recommend screening. Even men who are desperate for a urological test cannot get one because the tests themselves do not exist, having been deemed "cost ineffective." (Anal HPV tests do exist, however, and of course trans men with cervixes are also at risk.) The functional equivalent to a penile HPV test is a man repeatedly and exclusively having unprotected sex with a woman and then inquiring about her pap results. Even then, given the tendency of HPV to go dormant or to lie below the level of detection for years, it's often difficult to pinpoint the transmission with anything like the shrieking certainty I had leveled across the country.

HPV diagnostics is rife with unknowing, but only men rest easy in ignorance. That the same knowledge was bestowed or withheld based on reproductive differences seemed central to my questions about my body and its ethical relation to others. For men, we have decided, the burden of knowledge outweighs the benefits. A man who knows he is positive for high-risk HPV has merely acquired an impediment to worry-free living, a source of ambiguous stress with no direct benefit to himself. For women, on the other hand, the risk of cervical cancer, which is low but statistically significant, makes the burden of knowledge worth its weight. The knowledge weighed heavily on me, but so did a feeling of guilt surrounding my lack of disclosure, which I quickly came to see as a moral failing. I decided to retroactively inform my friend.

When I told him, he thanked me for the information but was unphased. He'd had an active sex life and said he'd been with women in the past with both types of HPV, a piece of information that convinced me of two things: most men with long sexual histories had exposures they would not tell me about, and my own disclosures would never be passed forward to the women who stood to benefit from them.

In fact, he said, he was relieved I had not told him.

"Why's that?"

"I probably wouldn't have been able to get hard. It's a real boner killer."

Ah. I was learning so much.

•••••••

My second nondisclosure was to a man with a far-reaching sexual network. The chance that he hadn't had HPV at some point was almost impossible. And while I understood that a vague surety that he'd had some kind of HPV at some point was not the same thing as my currently almost definitely having high-risk HPV, I did not tell this man anything about my HPV status.

He smoked cigarettes, and I found myself debating whether this diminished my culpability given the increased risk for throat cancer. Our relationship never had the makings of anything long-term, and when it eventually expired, I again felt that by not disclosing, I had committed the most egregious offense of my life. I resolved to do better.

The first time I shared my HPV diagnosis before having sex was on a drunken one-night stand. The stakes were low, but I still felt uncomfortable, as if I were rudely interrupting a good time with dire news. He could not have cared less and replied that when he was younger, he'd had what he called a "real STD"—something that required a trip to the doctor and a prescription. As he talked about this experience, I considered the possibility that, despite the potential of unmonitored high-risk genital HPV killing a woman and the assurance that low-risk HPV would definitely never kill anyone, most men were more concerned about low-risk HPV because the warts presented an aesthetic problem. I imagined a scenario in which an average American man had to choose between exposure to a high-risk strain of HPV that he might pass on to another woman—who in turn may have to suffer cervical biopsies, a LEEP, or even death from cervical cancer—and exposure to a low-risk strain of HPV that might put a few treatable bumps on his dick. I was fairly confident he would choose the former.

But of course, no criticism of male vanity and callousness could have been less warranted—by not disclosing, I had essentially made this choice for a man myself. I felt confident now that disclosure was the clear way forward, no matter the unbalanced access to information.

As I was nearing the end of my two-year "wait and see" window, I met a new man. The circumstances of his life were bizarre and poignant, and as he narrated a story about his childhood puppy being run over by the town mortician, I knew I was a goner—he told the best anecdotes I had ever heard. We'd talked on the phone a few nights before meeting in person, and by the time we tipped horizontal, I felt like I knew him better than men I had lived with for several years. So of course when the moment for admission came, I was open about having high-risk HPV. I didn't think he would bat an eye, having witnessed him some time before place his best estimate for former partners at one hundred women, a staggering fact he somehow pitched in a way that seemed natural.

When I told him, he said decisively that it was not worth the risk. He did not want to have sex.

I was surprised, but I didn't get upset and didn't push the issue. I respected his right to decline sex with me, as well as his past decisions to sleep with almost anyone who, like a former version of myself, kept her HPV a secret.

We stayed in touch and hung out on occasion. Eventually he moved to another part of the country, and I figured I would never see him again. But he came back for a visit once while I was in the process of moving. I had only an air mattress, and he wanted to lie down to rest. Finally, he asked me if I wanted to have sex.

"I still have HPV," I said.

"Yeah, I don't care."

On the evening he first declined to have sex with me, he told a few stories about how in his younger days, he'd smoked crack cocaine. After my first disclosure, I recalled, I'd been called a boner killer. After my third, I'd been deemed more dangerous than crack.

This time, I declined.

•••••••

When I got to the two-year mark of my positive HPV status, the guidelines for management of high-risk HPV had shifted. Yet another new doctor said, "We'll just keep monitoring. The changes are still low-grade. Maybe it will be clear next time."

At this point, I'd been having biopsies of my cervix taken every six months, a procedure that had become easier to tolerate physically than financially. I calculated that if I had just coughed up the thousand bucks for Gardasil at age twenty-six, not only would I likely never have gotten high-risk HPV, but in the long-run, I also would have saved approximately $3,000.

I continued asking every new doctor I saw what they thought about the "ethics of disclosure," using that phrase. A young doctor I liked very much, who drawled in a monotone similar to mine, shook her head when I asked. "I mean, it's everywhere. They're finding it under guys' fingernails."

Despite my desire for a clear medical and moral imperative, no doctor ever told me that I was obligated to disclose or that disclosure was the correct choice. Evidently, we were living in an HPV-tolerant age, a medical era in which eradication was the goal for the next, thoroughly vaccinated generation. For women nearing forty, like myself, the towel had been thrown in: "Everyone has it, so let's just check in periodically and make sure it doesn't turn into cancer." When I first told a friend, who'd had HPV herself, about my positive test, it felt rather like being welcomed into a club—she called HPV "the people's disease."

I had started telling all of my friends, both male and female, often in non sequiturs, about my biopsies, hoping that the information would travel widely and osmotically so that as many people as possible were aware that I had HPV, as if I were engaged in a public campaign to head off the requirement to speak up in a more pressing instant. For in the absence of definitive guidance, my own self-originating commitment to disclosure continued to falter. Over the now four-and-a-half-year period during which I had been monitoring my HPV, I had opted not to disclose to three men. I knew my doctors absolved me of my choices, but these omissions bothered me. I started to wonder what other people thought. Was I right to assume that HPV, either in spite of or because of its prevalence, was rarely disclosed? Was I a bad person nonetheless?

I found one thread on Reddit and one on MetaFilter and was surprised by the content, as the majority of responses listed reasons similar to mine about why HPV disclosure was pretty much pointless:

> My thoughts are that sexually active people would be better off assuming that everyone they sleep with could have it and take [appropriate] precautions. . . . If you start pressuring people to disclose . . . we'll end up in a situation where a few people who are trying to be diligent will . . . end up stigmatised by people who are uneducated on it.

> I have sex with dudes, who can't get routine HPV tests, so no, I don't expect them to know their status. I generally tell partners that I had abnormal paps in the past, but regard it as more of a "we are getting to know each other" than "mandatory health alert."

> I recently found out I have a strain of HPV. I was worried at first, but the gynecologist flat out told me it's not necessary to tell people. . . . She suggested it would be polite to tell future partners, but there was no need to contact past partners. THIS IS WHAT THE GYNECOLOGIST TOLD ME.

Of course, not everyone was as unconcerned. In one lengthy and mildly condescending reply, username Patientpolyamorist lectured original poster bumpylog, who'd had warts years ago and was wondering if he needed to keep bringing this up, on transparency. The worst comment I could find struck me as relatively mild: "You are a disgusting bastard, and people like you are the reason it's so common in the first place. YOU ARE MAKING THE PROBLEM WORSE, DUMBASS."

I also went searching in medical journals. For a study in the *Western Journal of Nursing Research,* clinicians surveyed patients recently diagnosed with HPV and found that the majority were unsure about whether they needed to disclose their diagnosis to future or current partners. The authors also noted with surprise that (1) there was "no relationship between transmission knowledge and disclosure beliefs" and that (2) "both disclosers and nondisclosers felt good about their decision." I even tried to do a little informal research myself and invited my friends to participate in a questionnaire I created. One-third of respondents were aware that they'd had HPV at some point, but only 12.5 percent had always disclosed. Over 95 percent had never had a partner disclose their HPV status to them, and only one respondent replied that a partner's disclosure of a positive HPV diagnosis would prevent them from consummating a new relationship. I was taken aback, though, that about 60 percent thought anyone with any sort of HPV was ethically obligated to disclose. But then again, I once would have said the same thing; 70 percent of the respondents had never been diagnosed with HPV.

The most insightful journalism I came across was a piece called "The Silent Shame of HPV," written by Emily Shire for *The Daily Beast*. In the article, Shire interviews several women about their experiences with diagnosis and disclosure. Most of the women who chose to disclose to their male partners had poor experiences when doing so: "He said he knew he didn't have it because he 'was tested,' never realizing that there isn't a regularly available way to diagnose men with HPV strains." One woman attempted to tell the young man she had been seeing, who replied, "But we used condoms," and then "literally hung up" on her. A friend of mine had a similar result when she tried to inform her partner when she first tested positive. He insisted he could not have given her

HPV, and because there was no test to prove to him that he had the infection, he stood defiant on plausible deniability. She said she regretted telling him and assured me that I should in no way feel troubled about my own silence.

•••••••

In my search for answers about the right way to exist with HPV, I often felt alone and confused, and in parallel, my body never resolved the issue of HPV either. I was among the unlucky one-fifth of women whose high-risk HPV refused to disappear, and I ultimately had to undergo a LEEP.

Before my loop electrosurgical excision procedure, I first signed several consent forms, one of which asked me to acknowledge that I understood the shortening of my cervix would increase my chance of miscarrying should I ever wish to bear children. A nurse then applied a sticky electrical ground to my thigh to prevent my being shocked should the machine malfunction, while inside my vagina. As my doctor numbed my cervix, she warned me that once we got started, the machine would whine like a loud vacuum, "to suck up all the smoke."

That an electrically charged red-hot wire would be dragged across my cervix, that the smoke of my own burning squamous cells would be hoovered away from me through a clear plastic tube—all this struck me as at once objectively horrifying and subjectively neutral. Shortly after the Wallach Quantum 2000 electrosurgical machine whooshed to life, I heard the crackling static of the wire. My doctor warned me and took her first pass. I'd been assured I would feel nothing, and while the sensation was tolerable, it was not nothing.

And then, in fact, the machine malfunctioned. The static buzzing went silent, and my doctor turned to fiddle with the wires and switches. Eventually she said, “The wire isn’t heating up.” While I lay splayed and speculumed, the wires were swapped out, until finally, my doctor readied me for the second raking. “This should just take two passes yet,” she reassured me. But as she pressed the searing wire against my flesh once more, my doctor looked on in amazement as the instrument, instead of passing through, simply bent in on itself like string.

That the wire was still insufficiently hot seems the likely cause of this second snafu, but the doctor suggested instead that my cervical tissue was exceedingly tough. I took it as a compliment, though in the end the procedure took about forty-five minutes and was quite unpleasant. Once, the wire brushed against unnumbed, noncervical tissue, and my body confusedly flinched in all directions. But finally—or so I was told—all the questionable tissue was excised and the healthy underlying tissue cauterized. When the lab results came back, the margins were clear. Now, presumably, I was HPV free.

• • • • • • •

I can’t help but view the mishaps during my LEEP as a cosmic punishment for my hesitancy. If I could do it all over again, which conveniently for me I cannot, I would disclose to the three men I consciously did not inform at the time. For me, complete disclosure would have been the right decision, the honest and open choice, despite knowing my partner would never know his own status and would possibly condemn me for mine. And while I don’t believe my decisions to withhold were wrong, they were not ideal, and I am an idealist.

I regret these decisions in a way I do not regret the sexual relationship, or possibly relationships, that gave me HPV in the first place. I am disappointed in myself for hiding something my ethical impulses said to reveal. I am not disappointed in myself for having had, and profoundly enjoyed, sex that had consequences.

My HPV diagnosis largely overlapped with my sexual peak, which was Himalayan, and this was both a blessing and a curse. In my early thirties, I wanted to have sex every day, but my concern about exposing others as well as the pressure to disclose and the guilt I felt when I did not led to entire six- and twelve-month periods of celibacy. The long days I spent treading water in that deluge taught me much about how to notice the body's needs without acting on them, a useful practice now that I am definitively HPV negative. I dread the prospect of a new infection, but given the exclusion of men from testing, my conclusive negative will be as one-sided as my probable positive once was.

And so I am back where I started—isolated in my knowledge, a position in which many women find themselves during some of the most significant events of their lives. From the obfuscation of menstrual realities to the lack of transparency in basic women's health procedures, from the private devastation of miscarriage to the open secret of abortion, many woman—as I do—know how it feels to be the lone learner in the schoolhouse of the body.

ALL THE DEAD DOGS

Let us begin with a disavowal. For as long as I once believed in God and lived among those who believed in God, I have now lived even longer not believing in God. At forty-one, the balance continues to tip farther from the divine—eighteen years of belief, twenty-three of disbelief. But this is the twenty-first century, and such an admission, I know, is uninspired heresy. It's far more controversial to say: I also no longer believe in dogs.

•••••••

Pilgrim, a black-and-white shepherd mix born on Thanksgiving, was our family's first dog, and he spent his younger years running loose on my grandparents' dairy farm, which we could see from the backyard of our little red ranch house to the west. Then work slowed down for my dad, and my parents had to sell the house they'd just built. For one year, we lived in an apartment where Pilgrim could not stay, and then we moved into the first floor of a large green house and brought him with us. My mom says our first mistake in our long history of ill-fated pet ownership was taking Pilgrim off the farm, even though the green house was itself technically a farmhouse. The property hadn't been operational for years, but it still had a cavernous barn, deep fields, and a shallow pond. Certainly, as on a real farm, plenty of animals died there.

Pilgrim getting a bucket bath.
Author's family collection.

Pilgrim was the first, though my family also cycled through other pet species—five rabbits, three hermit crabs, a cat, and a score or so of flushed fish. Once, I even raised a sheep for a 4-H project, a lamb destined for slaughter from the moment I chose her. But Lambers ended up winning a state fair and retiring as a breeder, so somehow, the animal I had raised for meat fared better than any of our pets.

My mom babysat, and Kyle, one of the kids who stayed with us after school, had a habit of hitting Pilgrim, despite our requests that he leave the dog alone. One week Pilgrim developed an ear infection, and Mom emphasized to Kyle that he needed to be gentle, or better yet, not touch Pilgrim at all because his ear was sore. Kyle's mother came to pick him up, and while she and my mother chatted, Kyle stood by the refrigerator poking the dog.

His own mother turned to him. "Stop it, Kyle."

And then with a loud bark, Pilgrim lunged and bit Kyle in the face. The bite was nothing grisly, but the shallow puncture wounds bled fast enough to scare everyone. Kyle was back to normal within a week. Whole again, he went to his grandparents' house and walloped on another dog, who sank his teeth into Kyle's arm.

By this time, my parents had already, agonizingly, put Pilgrim down. It's unlikely this second incident would have changed their minds. Kyle's parents had not made any particular demands, but my own parents, who doubtless also worried about their continued babysitting liability, had a long-standing agreement that a child-biting dog would not be tolerated. I think when they had contemplated such a scenario, though, the imagined child was one of their own and the circumstances less ambivalent. They'd had Pilgrim longer than they'd had us.

Pilgrim certainly hadn't resembled the biting dogs of my childhood, which were either rabid (*Cujo*), misunderstood (*The Sandlot*), or demonically reanimated (*Pet Sematary*). No, in his starring role, Pilgrim appears on VHS at an Easter dinner on the farm when my brother was just a baby and Pilg was about seven. As Pilgrim winds his way through the picnic table legs, my dad plops my brother onto his shaggy back, bouncing PJ up and down, and our family dog stands with his tongue out, tail wagging. My parents could not have been more shocked when this same dog later snapped his teeth through the skin of a child's cheek and forehead.

Pilgrim was not an aggressive dog. But he was a dog, a powerful, unpredictable thing we had brought into our home, for better or worse. Because my first dog was unexceptional in every way until one day he bit a child in the face and was subsequently destroyed, I have been an uneasy member of the church of dog from the start, doubtful of its main tenet, that despite the inevitable foibles of human-dog communion, redemption abides. Already prone to stray in matters of dogma, I've recently been reading and watching widely, trying to make sense of the American family dog and to account for my family's life with ours. One of the first books I picked up was *How Dogs Work*, by Raymond Coppinger and Mark Feinstein. I'm not sure what tally Pilgrim's bite counted toward in 1989, but the annual number of dog bites has risen significantly in the decades since. Coppinger and Feinstein put it at 536 Americans every hour, about 4.7 million people a year, and go so far as to claim that dog bites are "the second largest public health problem" in the country.

Once, hoping to find a fellow apostate, I clicked on an article titled "There's No Such Thing as a Good Dog." But I'd been baited, and the article's thesis was merely a reversal of the adage "There are no bad dogs, only bad dog owners." The good ones too, the article suggested, are purely products of human creation. I think this is only partly true, but I also won't fight the implicit charge. If consensus says Pilgrim bit Kyle after weeks of tail and fur pulling because my family didn't train him not to, I'd only suggest that in our guilt, in our admission of having been bad dog owners, we cop to a fault that is practically universal.

• • • • • • •

Our second dog was an enormous collie named Kodie. He was beautiful and riotously affectionate. A few times, he came to visit me during recess at my elementary school a mile away from home. Having lived in urban areas for nearly two decades now, the relaxed attitude toward leashing where I grew up seems almost impossible to comprehend, but indeed, we often let our dogs run loose. Kodie

Kodie and me and the endless field in back. *Author's family collection.*

ran around so much, he was something of a community mascot, once appearing as an unplanned guest in the local marching band's halftime show.

Of course, one problem with dogs running loose in the country is that they are frequently hit on the road. We tended to think of Kodie as invincible after he'd plowed straight into the side of a moving vehicle and walked away less shaken than the driver, but this luck didn't last. After he was hit and killed by a truck driven by the father of a school friend, Kodie became the first dog we buried in the sacred pet cemetery on the hill by the pond. Pilgrim had been buried on my grandparents' farm, and I was not there to see it. With Kodie, we all trudged out behind my dad, who pushed the wheelbarrow over the stiff weeds, Kodie's body wrapped in a black trash bag.

Another dead dog, and what, in addition to the body being covered with earth, had we ruined this time? Two cars, a man's ride home, a marching band.

Still, I think if dogs were given a choice—if dogs could evince such choices in some way other than leaping over every obstacle between them and freedom—to run in traffic or be stuck behind apartment walls, I wager most dogs would take the traffic. Unlike me, whose grown-up discomfort with dogdom still owes much to risk aversion (at dog parks, I stand nervously, awaiting a bloodbath), dogs do not, I believe, long for the safety Americans delimit for them. If you listen, through your walls or across the yard, they seem to be telling us as much—and pretty emphatically.

Every building I have occupied since leaving home has been adjacent to several cooped-up or tied-up dogs lamenting their circumstances. Free-roaming dogs bark far less often than dogs whose movement is restricted, and Coppinger, along with his wife, Lorna (also a dog researcher and collaborator), argues that the constant barking of fenced and leashed dogs is due to their inability

Kodie and me and the road in front. *Author's family collection.*

to either flee or pursue. The church of dog has a Catholic bent, as the eternal state of most American dogs is purgatory.

When I'm not being serenaded by barking, I'm instead listening to the cries of dog owners, petulant commands bellowed in the direction of an unresponsive animal I can neither see nor hear. "JAKE! . . . JAAAAAKE! JAKE!! WHAT ARE YOU DOING?"

"JAKE!"

"NO!"

"JAKE!"

"JAKE!"

"GET OVER HERE!"

These performances, among the most abject monologues I have ever witnessed, go on for a long time, but they never end in an implosion of shame as I expect.

Americans violently disagree on the proper function of restraint in dogdom, and this debate becomes particularly unhinged, I think, because dogs cannot speak. Instead, dog owners fancy themselves advocates for the verbally defenseless, projecting their own desires and delusions about freedom, responsibility, entitlement, and the rule of law onto animals we've placed in rather tricky environments.

To wit: I once dated a libertarian who didn't register his dog, didn't vaccinate his dog, and took her wherever he liked, often off-leash. On an outdoor restaurant patio, whose rules regarding dogs he had not bothered to inquire into, his dog pulled her leash to its maximum and sniffed around the legs of other restaurant goers, who tolerated her, while I, having witnessed enough awkward encounters over such presumption in the days since Kodie, worried and complained. When a friend of mine took her toddler to a public park where dogs were required to be leashed and asked a woman whose dog was bounding toward her son to please tie it, the woman called her a bitch and a bad mother and berated her for several minutes. In a marathon group, I used to run alongside a cop who trained police dogs, and one evening he brought his pet dog, a large, intimidating creature who was in no way identified as a service dog, into the YMCA, where it made a beeline toward a young boy. When the boy leapt up into his chair to get away from the dog, the cop was snide, suggesting his reaction was uncalled for and had invited trouble. Recently, a sheriff's deputy in this same state went to serve a divorce summons, and when a German shepherd of the same size and build moved toward him, the deputy shot the dog in the face. Catty-corner to my house, my neighbor's German shepherd lunges at everything that passes, straining at a poorly secured ground pin, and when walkers express dismay, my neighbor shouts and swears at them. I know the pin is poorly secured, because other nights, I listen to this neighbor drive around the block calling out her dog's name: "Skyler! Come on, girl! Where are you?" At a bog at 4 a.m., my own mother, who still believes a dog can't fully be a dog if it lives its whole life on leash or behind a fence, used to walk dogs number eight and nine to avoid a bird-watcher who had reported her to the ranger for letting the dogs run loose; they set pheasants bursting out of the brush.

I couldn't fathom my mother's anger at this woman, whose complaints seemed justified. But dogs frequently enable their owners to tell themselves, when rules are bent, that the disobedience is not on their own behalf. And besides, who doesn't love a dog?

Well, now that dogs are unavoidable, more people than you think, though even mild criticism of dogs (whose sense of self, I feel compelled to point out, does not derive from discourse about them) is sometimes cast as an unforgivable position, a pathological deviance. In an episode of *It's Always Sunny in Philadelphia,* centered on the gang's efforts to outpace bad publicity in the twenty-four-hour news cycle, Dennis, your friendly neighborhood deviant, manages to twice redeem the damaged reputation of Wolf Cola, only to finally be undone by his televised disdain for dogs. Of course, in typical *Sunny* fashion, Dennis takes things a bit further and ends by suggesting he should be able to eat a bucket of dog: "All I'm saying is . . . let's be *consistent*." Below, live tweets scroll by:

> @doug_thorburn: WTF?!?! Who doesn't like dogs?
> @ThePaoMuchacho: Is Wolf Cola ANTI-DOG!?!?!
> @Lseggy: F Wolf Cola and F this guy #forthepuppies

I'm not ready to say I dislike dogs. I like most dogs in the right environment well enough, and most dogs, though not all, have liked me.

• • • • • • •

Our sorrow for Kodie was such that we immediately replaced him with not just one but two new dogs. We named these Akita mutts Taylor and Dayne, in homage to the crimp-haired alto popular at the time. Akitas were historically bred in Japan to hunt bears, and despite the fact that my mom walked them constantly and they had plenty of room to run, from the start, these were two high-strung, aggressive dogs. Our sister Akitas fought with each other so much we eventually put them on two separate runs attached to trees at opposite ends of the backyard. Feeding them required tactical maneuvering, and the operation went like this:

(1) Child 1 runs like mad through the center of the dogs' range, which causes the dogs to come tearing toward her from opposite ends of the yard.
(2) While the dogs are in carnivorous pursuit of child 1, child 2 swoops in to grab the food and water dishes under Taylor's tree.
(3) Child 2 empties and fills the dishes with fresh food and water, then waves to her partner, who stands panting out of the dogs' reach across the way, to indicate that she is ready to return the dishes.
(4) If the dogs are still busy strangling themselves on the ends of their runs, child 2 returns Taylor's dishes. If the dogs have returned to their shady spots under the trees, child 1 repeats step 1 in the opposite direction.
(5) All steps are repeated for Dayne, with children switching roles.

"Love, love on the run!"

I have no memories of playing with these dogs, no recollections of sopping tennis balls returned to my hand, and when I think of

Taylor and Dayne, I confess to being charmed by certain uber-rational, profoundly skeptical, and refreshingly heretical takes on the very notion that dogs play, or at least play in the romantic and anthropomorphic sense we like to think they do. My favorite comes again from Coppinger and Feinstein in *How Dogs Work,* where they claim that many of the activities we categorize as "play" are in fact incomplete behavioral sequences short-circuited by the circumstances of domestication:

> Like a piece of ill-written computer code that can't terminate, a playing border collie or a young wolf that hasn't developed the full sequence [of stalk, grab, kill, dissect, consume] simply goes back and starts over. This is nonfunctional and energetically very expensive activity to be sure, but . . . incomplete or even maladaptive behavior can be a satisfying activity. . . . The bottom line is that we can view play as an emergent consequence of the expression of a developing repertoire of motor patterns that are not yet fully functional.

Think on *that*—that all the playful exuberance we value in dogs might be the result of a glitch, the inability to reach the "functional end point" (dissect, consume) of a hardwired canine motor sequence pattern.

One day I invited my friend Adrianne over to our house, and on the bus ride home, I regaled her with tales of Taylor and Dayne's ferocity. We hopped off the bus and ran to the backyard, where we found the metal clasps at the end of the dog runs lying on the grass, no dogs attached. My mom, feeling terribly guilty for doing so, had given up and taken them to the pound.

I felt more embarrassed about having let Adrianne down than sad about their disappearance. Even as I say this, I am surprised by my callousness. In my memories of these dogs, they did not act out the doggy behaviors that signaled "affection," so we withheld our emotional investment. As the grandchildren of farmers, we were accustomed to a moral world in which one opted in with certain animals and opted out with others. We were not, as Dennis Reynolds would complain, consistent.

•••••••

Gracie came next. Gracie was a blue merle Australian shepherd mix with eyes like constellations. She was the smartest of all our dogs and very fun to play with. Like Kodie, she was known to wander but not as often or as far. One night, though, she didn't come back. The next morning, Mom stood at the edge of the field and belted out her forlorn line—"Gracie!"—licking her lips when her whistles ran dry. Finally, she threw up her hands, distraught, and said, "There goes another dog."

Usually when Mom made such a prediction, our dog showed up a few hours later, covered in mud. But this time, Gracie did not come back—she simply disappeared. For dog number five, we held no solemn interment and were left instead to ponder grisly endings. A question mark lingered in place of instructive and tolerable finality.

After Gracie, we allowed ourselves a redo. We brought home another blue merle puppy, Hallie, and this time, we put an end to the unsupervised field trots. Hallie got run over anyway—twice—though she survived the accident.

That morning, Hallie was hit by two separate cars traveling in opposite lanes. My sister had let her outside before school, and when Mom ran out to scoop up the yelping dog and rush her to the vet, she was bit hard on the hand. After taking X-rays, the veterinarian relayed the surprising news that he could probably

Gracie briefly in the limelight. *Author's family collection.*

put Hallie back together, as all the damage was skeletal. My parents felt terrible for the dog, and they also worried that my sister would never forgive herself. So my parents, who did not have much money to spare, forked over $2,500 to reconstruct Hallie's hip. A few days later, she came home, her back half bristling with crooked stitches. She was still young, and she miraculously recovered without even a limp.

After all that, the death of dog number six was a matter of mere accounting. When Hallie was around seven years old, she developed an incurable skin disease and started gnawing at her paws, trailing blood around the house. A treatment existed, but it was only palliative. Faced with mounting vet costs, my parents crunched the numbers and said enough—we have spent enough on this one. And just like that, the last dog of my youth evaporated, run down by the bottom line.

Low-end estimates for the cost of owning a dog over its lifetime add up to $15,000, high-end estimates reach $40,000, and the

Hallie after a swim in Sugar Creek. *Photograph by the author.*

extravagances of some pet owners are hard to swallow in a nation where over ten million children face food insecurity. Not only can I not afford a dog, but I am also unwilling to occupy the inevitable position my parents found themselves in more than once—that of weighing a life against a bank account.

On the farm, my grandparents' dogs grew slow and tired until they wandered off into the woods to lie down and die. My family has never had a dog die of natural causes.

•••••••

Except for Kodie and Duncan, the dog that followed Hallie, all of our dogs were mutts. I was coming home only for the summers when my parents and my brother got Duncan, a purebred golden retriever whose favorite pastime was swimming into lakes to retrieve floating Milk-Bones. Duncan lived in five different houses while my parents tried to decide whether they should continue living together. During this time, my parents also took in my sister's dog, Meg—a muscular fluffball my sister had adopted after her own marriage fell apart—after Erin joined the Peace Corps.

Around age five, Duncan started having grand mal seizures. My parents put Duncan on medication, which initially helped and then helped less. They had to keep increasing the dosage, which exacerbated an unfortunate side effect—increased aggression toward other dogs. He was still having multiple seizures a day, and they were painful for my parents to watch, though they did watch them, and for a long time. Duncan's quality of life continued to deteriorate while his aggression continued to escalate, until finally, my parents agreed that he needed to die. My dad had been the one to take Pilgrim and Hallie to be euthanized, so my mom decided that this time, she would bear the burden.

Duncan the puppy. *Author's family collection.*

The night after she put Duncan down, my mother got black-out drunk and was kicked out of a bar. We are lucky no other disaster befell us the night of our seventh dog's death.

• • • • • • •

Duncan the dog. *Photograph by the author.*

In one of my favorite comedy sketches, Amy Schumer, Rachel Dratch, and Maeve Higgins, having dropped off their dogs at daycare, fall into bragging about their dog-children, which is primarily a form of bragging about themselves. The less desirable the dog, the more virtuous the owner: as Maeve Higgins's character explains, "My Duke, he was fourteen when I rescued him. His owners had just dropped him off at the shelter to die, and I was like, 'Nah uh, man. You're coming with me.'"

The absurdity of the rescued dog scenarios blossoms until a smartly dressed woman arrives holding a limp mass of fur and says, "Okay, Daisy, back at daycare."

Even the extreme dog moms are taken aback. "Is your dog dead?" Amy asks.

"Yeah," the woman replies, self-assured, "they just put her down at the pound about a month ago, and I was like, '*I'll* take her.' I was just doing what any hero would do, but she's my hero."

In today's dog-rescue parlance, "heroes" abound, but the term means something quite different than it did in dog cultures of our past. In her biography of Rin Tin Tin, Susan Orlean traces the early history of dogs in film and television, and she suggests that dogs like Rin Tin Tin first appeared in film as "peerless" heroes. As dogs moved into postwar American households, however, Lassie became the new paragon:

> [Dogs] were not living in a shed in the backyard; they were living inside the house as part of the family. Before this, dogs had been ideal heroes because we knew them but we couldn't really know them. . . . But as more people owned dogs, shared quarters with them . . . dogs lost some of that mythic otherness. People began to know dogs more and idealize them less.

I find this argument convincing, and I think it's time we advance it into the late twentieth and early twenty-first centuries. The movie dogs of the last thirty years have been anything but noble. Instead, they have been defined by unruliness. Think of Tom Hanks in *Turner and Hooch*, returning to his apartment to find his cupboards ransacked, his soccer ball deflated, and his records chewed in half. Hanks, a police officer who spends most of the movie bombastically complaining in his underwear, surveys the damage and threatens Hooch, "That's it, I'm getting my gun!" Think of the St. Bernard montage in *Beethoven*, where scenes of the Newton children teaching their new puppy tricks are interspersed with scenes in which the rapidly growing dog ruins their father's life: Beethoven pees on a briefcase, befouls a rug, scratches up a door, and finally leads Dad by way of dirty pawprints up to the bedroom for his iconic muddy shake. *YOU.*

And then of course we have *Marley and Me,* a film based on the real-life dog from the book of the same name. Perhaps the only thing worse than Marley the dog is the book *Marley and Me*. Aside from the saccharine and unsophisticated treatment of dogdom, John Grogan's sexual politics are very icky: between accounts of chewed drywall and shat out jewelry, you'll also learn precisely how attractive every woman Grogan encounters is, from the "homeliest hookers" he has ever seen to a "strikingly gorgeous makeup artist" and an underage stabbing victim he subtly sexualizes. His description of teenage sex workers is worth quoting in full: "We were approached . . . by two young women, teenagers really, who both looked strung out and nervous. Unlike the first women we had met, they were not terribly attractive and had taken no efforts to make themselves more so. They both looked desperate for their next hit off a crack pipe."

The film version of *Marley and Me* stars Owen Wilson and Jennifer Aniston, whose characteristic vapidity is appropriate. If you manage to finish *Marley and Me,* the treacly, bestselling lesson that awaits is that dogs instruct us to seize the moment, follow our hearts, and appreciate the little things. I'm not sure the hassle of Marley was worth the sentiments of a coffee mug.

If idealized dogs lived on the silver screen and family dogs occupied the television box, then the bad-dog movies of my childhood anticipated the tenor of reality TV, where "real people" like us fetishize problem(atic) dogs. The Amy Schumer sketch homes in on this paradoxical ideal, in which the most prized dog is now the most troubled, troublesome dog, but it is most fully realized in reality shows like *Pit Bulls and Parolees* and *It's Me or the Dog*.

My family, too, had come to believe in second-chance canines, and my parents' final dogs, dogs eight and nine, were shelter dogs. I say "my parents' final dogs," though both dogs started out as granddogs and were regifted by my brother and sister. Meg, whom we met earlier, and Moose, a medium-sized black-and-tan mutt, were adopted at three or four years old, their puppydom and dog adolescence a mystery. Neither of them could walk on a leash, and in the first few months of their cohabitation, they sometimes tangled each other into snarling, scratching tiffs that drew blood.

I knew very well how poorly Moose walked on a leash, for I had attempted to care for her for a summer. We enrolled in dog training courses and set out into the streets of Columbus, my first venture into an urban environment behind a canine. *My god,* I soon realized, *there are dogs everywhere.* In my halcyon pre-dog days, I hadn't noticed this density, for when I passed a dog on the sidewalk unaccompanied by another dog, the interaction was almost immediately forgotten. Maybe the dog had pulled on its leash to try to greet me or I had leaned down and extended

Meg was impervious to cold but terrified of storms. *Author's family collection.*

the back of my hand. Now I was one of two anchors opposing dog magnetism, and it seemed every fifteen feet, I was forced through a claw-scraping gauntlet.

I heard the woofing that punctuated these crossings as strings of profanity. "Hey!" Moose seemed to say. "Hey!"

"Hey yourself, asshole!" the other dog would reply.

"HEY! HEY! FUCK YOU!!"

"NO! NO! NO! FUCK YOOOOUUUUUUU!"

When Meg reached age ten, she became the oldest dog our family had ever owned. As she grew older, eleven, twelve, I found myself harboring a strange fantasy that one crisp morning, my parents would walk out to her doghouse and find her dead. What I mean to say is, I hoped that for once, a dog of ours would simply pass from the world naturally. But with both dogs, a year or so apart, my parents again chose to put them down when mercy was indicated. Mom and Dad were old hands at dog euthanasia by this time, but in recent years the procedure itself had undergone a transformation. Instead of making a final leap onto a cold examining table, the dogs were made to feel comfortable and relaxed, lying on blankets on the floor with Mom and Dad beside them. A whole memorial industry had burgeoned, with paw-imprinted clay tablets and carved wooden boxes for cremated ashes. And perhaps because Meg and Moose were sworn to be the last, and perhaps because these dogs had lived with them when their children were far away, Mom and Dad had

Moose was not the brightest.
Author's family collection.

Meg and Moose cremated and then set their ashes on the shelf. Enough years have passed now that I can say, with confidence and great relief, our life with dogs is over.

Receiving unconditional love from another is a rarely excusable neurotic fantasy. . . . [But] *the permanent search for knowledge of the intimate other, and the inevitable comic and tragic mistakes in that quest, commands my respect, whether the other is animal or human.*
—Donna Haraway, The Companion Species Manifesto

Inevitable comic and tragic mistakes indeed. In our life with dogs, my family made plenty, though I'm not confident all of them would have commanded Haraway's respect. Haraway, along with Mark Derr, is one of the great philosophers of the dog, and when referring to the human-dog relationship in *Companion Species,* she uses a series of phrases meant to capture a striving toward understanding across perceptual barriers: these include "the corporeal posture of cross-species respect," "otherness-in-connection," "situated partial connection," and "otherness-in-relation."

Truly, an ethics of togetherness that grapples with, instead of suppresses, meaningful embodied differences is among the most pressing questions of our time. I felt chastised, as I often do, when I read Haraway's generous appraisal of the efforts of dog owners, who after all are just trying their best to navigate shared living in the face of significant difference. In this light, my impatience with dogdom's missteps looks like a failure of empathy. When I read in John Homans's *What's a Dog For?* that "people who strongly dislike dogs score significantly higher on the measure of anal character and lower on the empathy scale of the California Psychological

Inventory," I immediately took several internet tests to determine whether I was anal retentive. I was not, the results suggested, but I tended toward perfectionism, and anyway, I don't "strongly dislike dogs." For a mild perfectionist, though, the chaos of loving a dog is a serious challenge full of contrary opinions fiercely adhered to. Practical advice for living out "cross-species respect" is sorely lacking in *Companion Species*, which Haraway acknowledges.

Many dog experts tell us that to treat a dog like a person is to do injustice to the dog, and while I think Haraway and Derr would agree, they are also interested in dogs as "category deviants," entities that constantly challenge strict boundaries. Derr rejects the notion of an "absolute divide . . . between the wild and natural and the domesticated and human-built." "No one," he says, "should be surprised that the dog bridges these worlds. . . . Yet ours is not a society that deals well with ambiguity, ambivalence, paradox, and border zones, and so the tendency is to cleave the dog from its wild side and lament the contradictions we have created. It is enough to drive a dog to ruin."

Certainly dogs, like humans, are richly paradoxical. For every complaint I've lodged here, one could swap in a story of a dog saving someone's life, not in an abstract sense but in a literal, dog-pulling-an-infant-out-of-a-burning-building sense. But we've already established that I am not an optimist. Even after being duped by "There's No Such Thing as a Good Dog," I am still prone to clicking on vaguely pessimistic dog-related ledes. In this way, I once came across a listicle of "least popular dog breeds," which condemned breeds for such defects as requiring "daily exercise" or being "non-hypoallergenic" or "not suited for apartment living." Even a dog skeptic should find these complaints preposterous, akin to criticizing a dog for requiring constant access to oxygen.

Sometimes I think our expectations for dogs are so out of sync with reality that we should abandon domestication altogether, but this thought not only makes me a close-minded category adherent but is also unlikely to be realized. I imagine as well my claim that most dog owners struggle mightily under the enormous responsibility of stewarding another life will be denied by many people. But success, I think, is the exception, and muddling the rule.

Perhaps my feelings about dogs are the opposite of my feelings about God. Regarding God, while the idea of divinity can be fun to play with, our realized version is not for me. Regarding dogs, while I find many of our beliefs about dogs to be misguided, manifest dogs can be fun to play with. So let us take a deep breath now and name them, all of my family's dogs, and see if we can't make it to the end: Pilgrim, Kodie, Taylor, Dayne, Gracie, Hallie, Duncan, Meg, and Moose. It is a litany to empty the lungs, enough to strain belief.

ORIGINAL SYNTAX

I once was a sinner on the road to Damascus who nitpicked my mother's speech. I persecuted her, crying "pattern!" when she noticed "a pattren" and "Saturn!" when she bought a "Satrun." But then my ears were opened, and when I heard "pattren" anew, I thought, *Wow—metathesis.*

I took up the study of linguistics on a whim, back when I was still a biology student who hadn't yet admitted that my real academic strength was language. I registered for an intro course as an elective and came into the class expecting it to be a higher-level study of sentence construction. By the end of the nine-week quarter, I expected, I would know every grammatical pitfall to avoid and every usage trend to decry.

Our first week of class was given over to first explaining what linguistics and linguists are *not*. I was shocked and somewhat chagrined to learn that first and foremost, linguistics is not the study of "grammar," by which I mean usage conventions of the prescriptive sort—do this, don't do this—hammered into us from a young age. Though the term *grammar* is often used in linguistics too, the object of study it refers to—how words are linked to form phrases, clauses, and sentences—is more commonly referred to as "syntax" and is decidedly free of value judgments. Further, *grammar,* as conventionally understood, is not only *not* the aim of linguistics—

as a methodology, it is frequently construed as the archnemesis of linguistics.

What, then, *isn't* a linguist? To be sure, a linguist is not a grammar snob, but she is also not a polyglot. Though most linguists work in at least one second language, their academic objective is not to learn as many languages as possible. They have the tools to do so, however, methodically and comprehensively.

In a matter of weeks, I was a convert. I did not want to be a language maven; I wanted to be a linguist.

As I started making my way through our textbooks, I felt enormous, fundamental misconceptions being dislodged from my brain in sensations that were nearly physical. Finally, we were learning what linguistics *is*: phonetics, phonology, morphology, semantics, and syntax, a set of interlocking subdisciplines that analyzes language from the ground up, from sounds to words to clauses. To begin, we needed to identify the smallest meaningful language unit. I thought I knew what the smallest unit was—a letter, right? But no, the smallest meaningful unit in any given language was something I'd never even heard of, a *phoneme*.

I'd spent most of my life studying language visually, on paper, while using it orally and aurally. In a refreshing reversal, our instructor told us that linguists treat human speech as the primary form of language, so writing systems—orthography—are considered tangential. Letters were a necessary conceptual stepping stone to phonemes, however, and so we began innocently with *a*.

In English orthography, this letter form can stand in for multiple "sounds." In elementary school, we were taught to distinguish two of them as "short a" (mat) and "long a" (mate), but of course *a* is pronounced in several other ways, such as in "all." Further, the same "a" sound quality—say, the "long a"—can be represented by different letters or strings of letters, as in "stake," "steak," and "stain." If we were aiming to locate the fundamental, discrete sound units in our language, English letters and their overlapping territories were not sufficient.

So, I was introduced to the concept of the phoneme, an idea at once so obvious and so surprising I felt as though I'd awakened from a long dream to realize I always had three legs. Phonemes are the unique, meaningful sounds on which all languages are built, and in American English, we use roughly thirty-six of them.

And now, if you'll bear with me for three paragraphs, we're going to get a bit technical. And then, I promise, it will all start to matter.

The method for determining whether a sound unit qualifies as "meaningful," whether it functions as a phoneme, is to verify its contrastive relationship with at least one other sound in something called a minimal pair: two words that vary in precisely one sound and, as a result of that variation and only that variation, mean different things. *Beet, bait, bet, bit, bat, but, boot, boat,* and *bot* are all minimal pairs. The words vary only on their internal vowel sounds and in this way demonstrate nine of our eleven distinct English vowels. *Bat, cat, mat, pat, rat,* and *sat* are also minimal pairs, varying only on their first consonant sound, as are *movie* and *moody,* varying only on internal /v/ and /d/.

To avoid the ambiguities of the alphabet, as well as to represent phonemes lacking a unique symbol, we learned to write words using the International Phonetic Alphabet. In IPA, the words *beet, bait, bet, bit, bat, but, boot, boat,* and *bot* look like this, respectively: /bit/, /bet/, /bɛt/, /bɪt/, /bæt/, /bʌt/, /but/, /bot/, and /bɑt/. I felt like a spy cracking a secret code, a code capable of unlocking the universe. In its fullest form, IPA can represent every known sound on Earth unambiguously. Yet learning the basics for English is a simple process that can be accomplished casually in a week or intensely in a day or two.

In English, every consonant phoneme can be distinguished from all others through three characteristics known as "distinctive features." For example, the phoneme /k/, as in the final consonant of "leak," can be fully differentiated from all other consonants in English through the description "voiceless velar stop." Change just one feature, and you get a different phoneme. Compared with /k/, /g/ shares the same *place* of articulation (velar, at your soft palate) and *manner* of articulation (stop—you briefly block the flow of air, build pressure, and then release), differing only in its *voicing*. Because your vocal cords are vibrating when you pronounce it, /g/ is a *voiced* velar stop, a new phoneme giving you a new word, "league."

The phoneme eng, or /ŋ/, as in the last sound in "ring," is also a velar consonant, and here, with our tongues jammed into the backs of our mouths, we leapt from the granular lessons of articulatory phonetics to the social implications of sound. Because the "ng" sound is spelled with two letters, many speakers of English mistakenly believe that to pronounce the final consonant in a word like "walking" as "walkin" is to "not pronounce" or "leave off" the "g sound" and as such is an expression of sloppiness, a speech pattern indicative of someone who "can't be bothered" to "say all of the letters." But of course, there is neither an /n/ sound nor a /g/ sound in "walking." The final sound in "walking" is a single phoneme, /ŋ/, a voiced velar nasal. To make this sound, you first block the passage of air through your mouth by lifting the back of your tongue against your soft palate, and then you let air escape through your nose while vibrating your vocal cords.

Even in light of this fact, people might erroneously insist that /ŋ/ is "correct" here, while /n/, a voiced alveolar nasal, is "incorrect," but as Mark Liberman explains in "The Internet Pilgrim's Guide to g-Dropping," "dropping the 'g'" was historically the more "conservative" phonetic pattern, diverging *less* from the earlier present participle forms -inde and -ende. And indeed, after -ing became a thing, people spoke of not "*adding* the 'g'" as a sign of high-class speech.

At one point in the article, Liberman, who is a linguist, laments that even "intellectuals . . . can't describe the basic facts of language in a coherent way," because they are never taught. Indeed, once you have a basic grasp of phonetics and phonemics, arguing about the relative values of accents and alternate pronunciations with people who lack this insight feels a bit like arguing with flat-Earthers about space flight.

• • • • • • •

Twenty years later, I still know that the sounds /p/ and /b/ are called bilabial stops, and I am unlikely to ever forget. And while I am not a language maven, I confess to a similar awareness concerning comma splices and an ability to speak at length about the distinct uses of the em dash and the en dash. Most people have never heard of a velar stop or an en dash, and somewhat strangely, the more likely you are to know and care about one, the less likely you are to know and care about the other, owing to the ties each has to distinct and sometimes antagonistic specializations.

On the big pond of academia, I'm an odd duck. Unable to settle on which approach to language I liked best—scientific, critical, or expressive—I am an almost linguistics major, a near PhD in literature, and an MFA who spent most of those years thinking about narrative theory. And so it is, one might say, that I have competing methodologies when I come to work every day as a book editor at a scholarly press. I must balance my descriptive heart with my prescriptive mind and my despairing soul.

The issues that grate on me as a book editor are not the usual suspects. My complaints are not about:

"Hopefully" as a sentence modifier—hopefully, you'll shut up about this because *of course* "hopefully" can be used as a sentence modifier, just as "thankfully" can.

Comma splices—of course I notice them, but a maven's aversion is a recipe for disaster. I was once aghast to discover a copyeditor had replaced all the comma splices *in character dialogue in a novel* with semicolons. Semicolons in dialogue!

Split infinitives—the proscription against split infinitives comes from a centuries-old campaign to make modern English mimic Latin, in which the infinitive attaches to the verb and cannot be separated. The present form of the English infinitive is made to be easily split.

Dangling modifiers—I usually reconfigure dangling modifiers when I spot them, but their egregiousness varies; some feel like running into a brick wall, while others are subtle enough to slip below the notice of people paid to fix them. Mostly, I find dangling modifiers to be funny: "Narrated by a different character in every chapter, Steven King creates a memorable tale."

"Comprised of" not meaning "made up of"—"comprised of" is such a shibboleth in copyediting I take a perverse pride in never quite remembering how to use "comprise" "correctly."

"Since" not meaning "because"—even *The Chicago Manual of Style* says this insistence is a fusty imposition.

Singular they as "illogical"—go fuck yourself.

Mostly, grammar school concerns like "don't split infinitives" are not what copyeditors are worrying themselves over either. Instead they're trying to ensure that the names of real people and places are spelled correctly; that claims are rational and do not contradict one another;* that basic conventions, such as book titles being placed in italics and articles titles in quotation marks, are observed, as these practices do make the next person's research just a little bit easier;† that citations in the notes line up with entries in the bibliography; that the meaning of the words on the page is coherent; and that the manuscript is made up of sentences.

Exploded constructions hoping to be sentences appear at an astounding rate. Take this one: "This concept is characterized by a resentment that results from the absent genius, which what anonymous writer craves most is recognition, but the problems specific to literature is that it lacks a dominant criteria." Or this one: "After the Elmo Society and the advice of the Great Debate decided to send Rev. Jacob F. Pike, of the Ohio Conference, for a trip to Washington and South Carolina." Or how about: "Our research examines voices who reflect and write about populations, migratory movements and navigate geographic and embodied places." From my side of the desk, an uncomfortable irony is ever present: the supposed experts in written language are failing spectacularly at it behind the scenes.

For despite the optimistic acknowledgements I sometimes see thanking the editor who contracted the book for her final "proofread" of the pages, almost all of our manuscripts are returned to the author by an underpaid copyeditor who has wrought upon

---

* A recent existential puzzle: "To protect her identity, Joan is a fictional character."

† Many scholars seem intent on writing a mystery novel in their notes citations, as the same work often appears in different guises across four consecutive notes:

1. Lee, "Getting It Right," 12–13.
2. Leee, *Getting it Write* 18.
3. Lee, 'Getting It Rite?," 15.
4. Lees. Getting It Wrong. pp. 12-14

One wonders: Are these clues pointing me to a book? An article? What's its *real* title? The reader may never know.

the pages a thicket of deletions and additions and queries. Some of these changes are to arbitrary matters of house style—adding serial commas, spelling out numbers. But many are repairs to serious errors in the text itself—its sentences, arguments, and documentation.

The redemptive impact of copyediting on most manuscripts is hard to overstate, and sometimes I think that if the six graduate students who read the final product were to read the original submission instead, the entire edifice of humanities scholarship would crumble. We'd all have to reckon with the fact that, for example, a world-renowned historian is under the impression that all punctuation marks are preceded by a space. That he inserted these spaces before every period, question mark, quotation mark, comma, and exclamation point in his seven-hundred-page manuscript.

Many days at work, I feel like Anders, the jaded literary critic in Tobias Wolff's "Bullet in the Brain," a man "known for the weary . . . savagery with which he dispatched almost everything he reviewed"—Anders, who gets his brains blown out because he can't rein in his disdain for bad dialogue during a real-life bank robbery.

I often sit at my desk unable to conceive of how human civilization came to be or still exists. Sometimes, I condense my obscure, protracted editorial complaints into haiku:

His magnum opus—
nine years! Still, chapter 2 has
three endnote fifteens

Behind every page,
hidden sins of formatting,
black pilcrow shows all

Dingleberry terd,
a modifier dangles,
cut off from its source

Last, late-breaking change,
name struck from acknowledgements,
quiet, red good-bye

Pink-cheeked expertise,
cracks in the ivory tower,
long, naked parade

Once, I submitted a few of these haiku to a work contest and won a gift certificate. The next contest, which asked us to recreate our favorite book covers and share them, added a new imperative: "Please keep it positive."

• • • • • • •

As in the jump from velar nasals to high-class "g" abstainers, linguistics moves from rote memorization to the big questions quickly—questions about how minds carve up words and worlds. Because while a phoneme is the smallest meaningful unit in a language, many phonemes are actually higher-level *abstractions* of several uniquely realized physical articulations. These variations, called "allophones," fly right under our meaning-making radar. Take /t/ for example. Say the words *top, stop, water,* and *mitten.* Don't overarticulate them, by which I mean, don't change anything about how you would normally say them in running speech. In a brain filtering for American English, all of these words contain the phoneme /t/, but most US Americans will pronounce these four t's in completely different ways in these word environments. The first /t/ is typically going to be "aspirated," which means accompanied by a little puff of air, which you can feel if you hold your hand in front of your mouth while saying "top." In granular phonetic, as opposed to phonemic, description, this sound is represented [t^h]. *Stop* normally yields an unaspirated version of /t/, without the puff of air. Now *water*, for me, and probably for you if you're being honest, is a weird little tongue tap on the top of my mouth. This is called an alveolar flap and is represented with the symbol [ɾ]. Now the shocker: for *mitten*, unless you have a hyperarticulated, "true" /t/ (which some people indeed do), your middle "t" is probably nothing more than an absence of sound, a brief closure of your vocal cords, a tiny choking action called a "glottal stop." If you don't have this sound in *mitten* or *kitten*—I have it in the name of my own hometown, Dalton—you certainly have it in "uh-oh." These variations of /t/ are known as "allophones."

So what do we even mean by a "t" sound given this evident variety? Linguists would say herein lies the distinction between [phonetic realizations] and /phonemic interpretation/. Just think, all this time, you've been saying "t" four different ways, two of which don't even resemble Mr. T's tall teeth, and yet you've been interpreting them all as /t/. Why haven't these other t's gotten their own names and Letter People characters (Mr. Glottal Stop, uh-oh!)? And how do we know your brain is lumping them all under an ur-/t/?

Because allophones can't form our old friend, the minimal pair. You can pronounce "water" with an aspirated /t/, an unaspirated /t/, or even a glottal stop, and an English speaker is still going to hear "water." Perhaps more to the point, you can't form any *new* words in English by substituting one of these /t/ variations for the other.

But in some languages, an aspirated /t/ and an unaspirated /t/ are separate phonemes—they're as different as /t/ and /d/ and can be contrasted in minimal pairs akin to "tip" and "dip." Aspiration, which also occurs allophonically on /p/ and /k/ in English, is a distinctive feature in Lakota, Korean, Icelandic, and Armenian, among other languages. Because aspiration is largely a subconscious distinction in English, training a monolingual English ear to pick out those little puffs of air as significant—as *the* feature that makes *this* sound different than *that* one—is a challenge. I had only ever studied German and Spanish, and while both languages have sounds that do not exist in English, none of them required me to suddenly recalibrate what counted *as* sound in the way my discovery of aspiration did. Conversely, some phonemes in English are merely allophones in other languages, so a predisposal for cognitively equating two sounds that English strictly separates, such as /b/ and /v/ or /v/ and /w/, will sometimes contribute to a nonnative English speaker's "accent."

All over Earth, every day, the same streams of social and material symbols are being parsed at different points and into differently sized units by the mesh of human cultures. Think of color categories. Think of Indigenous species names regrouping Linnaean. Think of the Western music scale as it lumps the long, undifferentiated slide of a trombone into the fuzzy mental pockets of D, D flat, C . . .

• • • • • • •

Given that linguistics despises prescription but does not take written language to be its object of study, given that most grammar snobs are ill-informed about the actual functions and forms of language, and given that I am a writer and pseudolinguist who thwarts prescription for reasons both expressive and informed, what, finally, is the hill I have chosen to die on? What usage pet peeve keeps me up at night and erodes my faith in humanity as steadily and powerfully as the overflowing, unwashed yogurt cups in my old break room recycling bin, over which read a large sign saying, "PLEASE RINSE YOUR PLASTIC. DIRTY PLASTIC CANNOT BE RECYCLED"?

My lonely, embattled hill is something known as indirect quotation.* In speech, we use indirect quotation constantly, and we execute this embedding with no hiccups: "She said she never wanted to see me again." English speakers are adept at implementing and processing the shifts in person and tense that result from a direct speech utterance being reported as indirect speech: the listener understands that the original speaker actually said, "I never want to see you again," not "she never wanted to see me again."

The problem starts when writers try to do the same, perhaps because when writing, we are not subject to the limits of memory or breath or turn-taking or interruption or any of the other dynamic factors of conversational speech, and instead, in the wide, empty field of the page, set out to build clauses more complex than many of us can safely navigate. For these reasons and others, written quotation often fails where speech quotation succeeds, despite the plodding pace and constant review.

My nightmare begins like this. Mr. PhD in English opens up any given work of criticism or any given novel and decides to extract a previously copyedited sentence or set of sentences inside his own, wholesale but indirectly. He does so with blithe confidence, never stopping to consider whether everything in the quotation is truly necessary to making his point, particularly its pronouns, or to check if perhaps the original passage might require a little massaging in order to slip into his own. Why would he? He's used *quotation marks*.

---

* Parallel structure issues, in which authors struggle with thinking, writing, and to be consistent, are a close second.

Many authors deploy quotation marks in writing the same way bigots hope to apply the First Amendment to speech—as an overly simplistic delineation within which anything goes. Or perhaps, less abstractly, writers treat quotation marks like syntactic lube—capable of sliming any and all phraseology past the friction of previously established person and tense.

Some examples of how *not* to integrate quotations:

> Bill "was younger and thoroughly intimidated and I followed Jill's example." (The "I" here refers to Bill.)
>
> The fifty-nine-year-old auto body technician . . . drives for Lyft on Saturday nights, when "I take drunk people home." (Again, the "I" refers back to the third-person subject.)
>
> He went to great lengths to keep "the breed as pure as I could."
>
> Chris remembers that "My uncle was tall."
>
> Prior to traveling, he told a friend that "my hope was to pass Christmas in Canada."
>
> In the ninth inning, seven-all, an unsung Cleveland infielder hit a "fly ball deep into left-center field and it is . . . a *home run*!" Martin cried.
>
> This gap between hope and reality is best described by Michael Shore as, "The action betrayed the confidence of marines."

If you are seeing catastrophe in only some of these sentences, keep in mind that the established syntax requires that the first five indirect quotations (the last two involve disasters of direct quotation) retain their meaning coherently *without the quotation marks*. If you rewrite these sentences without the quotation marks, the problem becomes more obvious; also, in spoken English, we would not use these forms to quote someone else:

> He went to great lengths to keep the breed as pure as I could from the first.
>
> Chris remembers that My uncle was tall. ("My uncle" being *Chris's* uncle.)

Only some of our copyeditors correct these usages, and authors, oddly reluctant to welcome the original text to its new surroundings, often request to stet the edits.*

One way to sand down these rough spots, which feel like splinters in my eyeball, is to use brackets: Chris remembers that "[his] uncle was tall." But brackets can become ungainly. Often, you can simply begin the quotation later: "He told a friend that 'my hope was . . .'" could be "He told a friend that his 'hope was . . .'" instead. You can also elide clashes. Where the first-person "I" clashes with framing third-person "Bill," use an ellipsis: Bill "was younger and thoroughly intimidated and . . . followed Jill's example." Or you can break the quotation into multiple smaller segments sprinkled throughout your own line, assessing for and highlighting which terms are truly

* I imagine these clauses peeking through their quotation marks to find themselves transported across time and space into a forest full of strangers.

important in the original—if you enjoy building sentences, this process feels like playing a game of quotation Tetris.

If all else fails, you can simply change the construction to a direct quotation: As Chris remembers, "My uncle was tall." This is often the most elegant solution, and sometimes all that is required is to replace your pesky "that" with a comma: Prior to traveling, he told a friend, "My hope was to pass . . . ." Of course, writers struggle with the setup of direct quotation too, as illustrated in the examples of the infielder and the marines, which crash and burn magnificently.

To watch writers fail so completely in the task of quotation breaks my complex-compound heart. The experience of reading average scholarship prior to copyediting is one of sitting hopefully in an author's syntax train only to derail over and over again into a screeching, smoldering tangle.

The sixteenth edition of *The Chicago Manual of Style* treats the issue of indirect quotation in but two brief sections, presenting the rules as if they were sufficiently obvious to hardly bear mentioning. Under "Assimilation into the Surrounding Text," sections 13.11 and 13.12 note that when "incorporating fragmentary quotations into a text," one should "phrase the surrounding sentence in such a way that the quoted words fit logically and grammatically, quoting only as much of the original as is necessary" and "integrate tenses and pronouns into the new context."

But here is my somewhat unique dilemma: I can't sit comfortably with my own distaste, keenly aware as I am that in writing, as in speech, usage changes and is the result of a long-term push-pull from top and bottom. These clumsy forms are so common that by even the mildest descriptive measure, mine is a lost cause.

• • • • • • •

Syntax is the domain where ideas of "right" and "wrong" loom largest, but it wasn't until my third linguistics class, on language and culture, that I had the visceral experience of being told that something I have been saying my whole life is syntactically repulsive to almost all other English speakers. The usage in question is called the "needs construction" and is exhibited by a small number of speakers mostly in northeast Ohio and northwest Pennsylvania and likely comes from Scots-Irish. I'd grown up in northeast Ohio and used this construction multiple times a day. To almost every other English speaker on Earth, the utterance jolts as powerfully as "I are smart," but I had no idea it was unique or, more significantly, impossible and inconceivable in most dialects. My instructor, a white-maned former missionary who'd spent most of his adult life with a group of Maya people in Guatemala collaborating on a writing system for Maya-Mam, asked us one day to raise our hands if we "could say" the following. Ready? *The car needs washed.*

Of course, I thought, raising my hand. *Who can't say* that? But only about a quarter of the class raised our hands. Had we not been sitting in central Ohio, I may have been the only one.

I watched my classmates with unraised hands recoil. *What?!* they cried. *Nooooo, that's so wrong!*

But of course it wasn't "wrong"—their dialects simply lacked the option to form these constructions, which pair "needs" with a passive past participle. I can do it with "wants" too: *The dog wants walked.* What you must understand here is that *I* couldn't understand my classmates' *inability* to understand the needs construction, a formulation we might take as a convoluted but functional definition of a form's being "grammatical." The needs construction is grammatical in my dialect.

Only after years of pondering was I able to conceive of the knee-jerk *Yuck!* this construction elicits in a speaker for whom *The car needs washed* is not grammatical. Instead of "needs," I tried a synonym, "requires." Lexically speaking, I should have been able to make the substitution, but I couldn't. To my surprise and delight, *The baby requires fed* sounded very strange indeed.

The needs construction is so obscure, few people ever have the opportunity to hate on it, unlike "habitual *be*," which is one of the most deeply misunderstood grammatical forms in English today. Habitual *be* is most common in Black dialects of English and is subject to both basic misinterpretation and outright denigration. Most speakers of "Standard" American English don't grasp that when Bob Marley sings, "We be jammin," this clause is not equivalent to "We are jammin."*

Habitual *be* is an innovation in the aspect system of English, a system we use to indicate how events unfold over time and in relation to one another (think: past perfect *I had watched*, present perfect progressive, *I have been watching*). Speakers without habitual *be* can of course still signal repetitious activity by saying, for example, "We regularly jam," and the form's implication of a character trait can be conveyed through statements like, "We are the sort of people who jam," but speakers with habitual *be* encoded *in their grammar* can signal these meanings through a simple uninflected copula.

A lack of understanding concerning the different meanings of "is" and "be" in certain dialects can result in confusing, embarrassing, and sometimes punitive encounters between educators and students. A young speaker who can differentiate "is" and "be" but is forced to conflate the forms at school is sometimes being asked to make statements that are literally not true. Imagine a four-year-old

* Let me also lament that cross-dialectal confusion has led many dudes to insist that "No woman, no cry," rather than meaning, "No, woman, don't cry," is some sort of Men Going Their Own Way battle cry about the blessings of bachelorhood.

attends daycare while his mother works. On a given day, however, his mother is home sick. Now imagine that on that specific day, a teacher asks the student where his mother usually spends the hours he is at daycare, and he answers, "She be at work."

"Oh, she *is* at work," the teacher responds.

Well, no, she *is* at home.

In response to a similar exchange, an exasperated student cited in one study finally asked, "Why do you want me to lie?"

People attempting to ridicule habitual *be* often reveal their ignorance in the process, such that when Joan Rivers ironically dedicated her last book to Kanye West in the form, "This book be dedicated to Kanye West," she produced a truly ungrammatical utterance, an utterance that in all dialects of English would be preceded by an asterisk, the linguist's mark for "cannot be formed by a speaker of this language"—one cannot habitually dedicate a book. Unlike Kanye's original statement, "Sometimes people write novels and they be so wordy and self-absorbed," a fair assessment, Rivers's response is, objectively, wrong.

• • • • • • •

Sometimes, the descriptive part of my mind and the prescriptive part of my mind actually get to work together. For instance, at my first job in academic publishing, I spent hours testing and tweaking an inherited set of search-and-replace cleanups after witnessing how well-intentioned Word macros laid waste to Native language texts. With a click of one button, a tool that was intended to clean up common hyphenation mistakes introduced hundreds of errors into discussions of suffixes and prefixes. With the click of another, thousands of superscript phonetic markers indicating aspiration or glottalization fell to the baseline, where they now meant something else entirely. To be attuned to such wreckage, and to then be able to rewrite procedures to prevent it, was a rare moment in which my competing backgrounds complemented one another.

Indeed, to see an Indigenous-language dictionary or grammar through the standard book production process requires a kind of finicky, even maniacal expertise about diacritics and punctuation that I absolutely possess and that many people regard with suspicion. Once, after making a bemused observation among bookish people about how much of my job revolved around the difference between an em dash, an en dash, and a hyphen, I was taken aback when someone replied, "I hate it when people care about punctuation." The assumption, of course, was that anyone who *knew* that an en dash went between number spans must be the kind of person who *judged* you for using a hyphen instead, a monster who probably ended all of her texts with a period. In reality I was, like most people, full of contradictions, the kind of person who knew the rules of direct address and still opened emails *Hi Ellen*.

As someone who tries very hard to balance the advantages of language conventions with the conviction that they carry no inherent value, I felt extremely uncomfortable to have been measured, sifted, and summarily tossed out with the mavens. I thought about defending myself by mentioning that, in fact, one of my all-time favorite people adds apostrophes to all plural nouns in his written correspondence and how, were this aspect of his "text's" to ever affect my opinion of his intelligence, I would hate me too.

And then, of course, there was *speech*.* Since my first linguistics class, my ears had practiced a kind of rationalist loving-kindness

* And let's not forget signed languages. When I learned that ASL is not simply a transliteration of English, a one-for-one equivalency where ASL sign *x* stands for English word *y*, but instead a unique language in and of itself that encodes syntactic information very differently from English, my opinion of human beings hit an all-time high.

to spoken language I could only dream of applying to people as a whole. But how to convey, in a short space of time, the revelatory power of the aspirated [t^h] allophone? The existential decentering that accompanied learning my own dialect contained forms that were unutterable but for a few? The paradigm shift that allowed me to finally understand that even if Elmo has two Oreos in his mouth and Cookie Monster has none, Cookie Monster, not Elmo, be eating cookies?*

And yet this, too, is true: in the tiny gap of a letter space inserted before a period, I sometimes see the void .

•••••••

On occasion, in the middle of carping about commas or parallel structure or trainwrecked syntax, I become cognizant of the fact that I am poorly dressed. *Sharp dressers,* I chide myself, *probably despair over your sweatpants the same way you despair over indirect quotation.* But unlike a scholar who can't be bothered to spell his copyeditor's name right in the acknowledgements—gifting the innocent target of this gratitude with yet more work—I am not trying to publish a fashion magazine while wearing sweatpants.

Prior to the in-person interview for my last job, I sat in my sweatpants and read the entire *Chicago Manual of Style,* 860 pages of rules about hyphenation and table numbering. Shortly thereafter, at work, deep in the convoluted failures of an author-created book

* See Janice Eurana Jackson's 1998 UMass Amherst dissertation, "Linguistic Aspect in African-American English Speaking Children," in which she found the following: "The results of this study confirmed that AAE speaking children understand the targeted aspectual contours of aspectual 'be' and do not confuse aspectual 'be' with SAE regular forms of 'be,' but rather are able to identify aspectual 'be' as a separate additional lexical item (marking specific aspectual contours) in their linguistic repertoires."

index, I texted a friend who works as a nurse to complain, and he reminded me, helpfully, *Isn't your job basically polishing turds?*

And then I thought of Anders, the fictional literary critic. How all along his delight in language remained buried under the tarnish of years and mediocrity, at its core so pure that in his final moments, it shone brightly at last. As the bullet passes through Anders's brain, the old crank reexperiences his original enchantment. It is summer, and he is playing baseball with his friends. One of the players has brought a cousin from out of town, and from the visitor's mouth, young Anders hears something he's never heard before, and it is not a curse word or a song or a joke but a simple turn of phrase—"the best . . . they is." Anders stands in the outfield, repeating the words to himself, enraptured by their surprising music: *they is, they is, they is.*

I wonder, when my time comes, what phrase will be running through my mind as I go under. Maybe, if I'm lucky, I'll die thinking, *the car needs washed, the car needs washed, the car needs washed.*

WITH HOME

EVEN IN DEATH

In the country, there are bad roads—little county roads that intersect major highways at thirty-degree angles, gravelly, intestinal roads with wild grass bent over the berm. Roads that toss teenagers into trees. Where I grew up, kids were always sliding into Winnebegos or slipping on loose summer chip-and-seal, and then dying, despite the life flight to the city hospital.

They were usually jocks, driving home late from a game or weathering the Christmas break snows to get to the gym for practice. And their deaths—the mythical, enduring tragedy of an athlete dying young—helped build our sports facilities.

• • • • • • •

I got my Ohio driver's permit in 1999, at fifteen and a half, and shared a used blue hatchback Saab 900 with my sister. The Saab was hardly a common car where we lived, as the hour drive to the nearest dealer for repairs made clear, and it exuded sufficient personality to develop a high school fan club. In college, friends who came across other 900s would text grainy pictures captioned "Saaaaaab!" The only other car equally distinctive at school that fall was Brianne Hummel's Volkswagen New Beetle, but Brianne was the one ostentatiously rich kid in a school mostly made up of the quietly wealthy, deeply rural children of Mennonite entrepreneurs. Her vanity plate read "Humm Bug," and she threw her vending machine change down the hallway, where I usually ran after it. The Saab, unlike the Humm Bug, was cool without trying to be.

I liked the car because it was idiosyncratic—the ignition was on the floor between the driver's and passenger's seats, the hood slid forward toward the front bumper instead of popping up toward the windshield, and to get the car into reverse, you not only had to navigate through the usual stick-shift slot points (far right, straight back) but simultaneously pull up on a ring below the gearshift knob with your first and middle fingers. It was fun to watch guys search for the ignition, to grab the gearshift and show them the trick.

Knowing how to operate a manual transmission automatically makes you more awesome, but the learning curve is never smooth. For one week that summer, I peeled out / stalled out / threw my neck out in school / church / shopping center parking lots. I nearly killed myself and my mother only once. That day I stalled three times, my front end having subsequently lurched itself halfway into one of four lanes on Route 30, the highway behind our house. There, at the Kidron Road intersection with the cheese shop, the vet clinic, and the Bible camp, I idled in a panic until my mother yelled "Move!" and unbuckled her seatbelt. We opened our doors and ran, Hondas and Fords blowing by and tossing our hair. Mom started the car, moved forward an inch, and stalled. The car was in third gear.

When years later I asked my parents how we ended up with such an unprovincial car, without hesitation Mom said, "That thing was a tank."

Of course. My parents had bought the Saab for only one of its many distinctive qualities: safety.

• • • • • • •

In 1997, Mark Kiper, a nineteen-year-old basketball star who had made the jump from high school to small-time college—he was on the team at the College of Wooster, the only four-year college in our county—was struck and killed by a semi while working on an ODOT summer road crew on Route 30. In the summer of 1999, my brother, then entering the seventh grade, sweated through outdoor games on Mark's namesake basketball courts, himself one of the star players of the Mark Kiper Memorial Summer Basketball League.

"Mark Kiper was the kind of young man parents dream their son will become," an article written three years after his death tells us. "A National Honor Society member in the classroom and an all-district basketball player on the hardwood. . . . [, the] only things Kiper enjoyed more than basketball and school were family and tutoring younger children with sports and classwork." Along with the outdoor courts and the league, a concession stand was built with donations given in his memory, and a Christmas tree was planted. Mark's parents hung the tree with lights every December, and some seasons, these lights burned long after the first of the year so as not to jinx a hot streak. We dreaded any team playing in memoriam, fearing an uncomfortable victory as much as their unstoppable momentum.

Two winters after my brother started playing in the Mark Kiper League, I came to school and found my friend Laura crying in homeroom. When I asked her what was wrong, she quaveringly told me that Sara Cottrell had died in a car accident. I ushered Laura out of the room without asking permission, taking her to the library, where she continued to cry and I continued to ask questions, my usual response to shock. We'd known Sara through basketball, playing with and against her on various AAU club teams for four or five years. She was a point guard and sprinter with strong thighs, a twin brother, a mom with MS. Seventeen, she'd crashed head-on into an RV.

On a school day the next week, Laura drove me and another classmate to the calling hours in her purple Cavalier. She was the first of our friends to get a cell phone because she had a forty-five-minute drive to school. After Laura turned the engine off that afternoon, we sat in the strained sunlight while she called home and let her parents know we'd gotten there all right.

Sara's parents were not rich—there is no Sara Cottrell memorial gymnasium, no Sara Cottrell track and field scholarship. Though her family was eventually awarded $400,000 in damages, the only public legacy I can locate is a 2001 newspaper article about a high school track meet in which Sara's former coach cites her death as inspiration for their victory.

•••••••

In the tiny school district I attended for elementary and junior high school, it seemed as if every class, about seventy students, experienced exactly one death. In my class it was Brian Slates, the first boy I ever had a crush on, who died not in a car accident but of cancer. I came in through the north doors one morning and gathered with my classmates under the track and field record board, a board where my dad still appeared, my brother would soon arrive, and even I, for one brief, glorious season after the 200-meter hurdles were introduced as a new event, was to be found. And there was Rachel Hayes, crying.

"Brian died."

Downstairs in the locker room that day, I watched one of my closest friends, a different Rachel who would make it all the way to college with us before perishing in a car crash in western Ohio, weep and kick the lockers violently and repeatedly. I walked to the pay phone and left a collect call message for my mother, who arrived in the lunchroom to hug me.

I remember with great clarity how at the calling hours, my father, who knew Brian through coaching basketball, reached up to touch Brian's parents on their shoulders and how the tall pair leaned down to him to hear what he had to say. My father shook as he spoke: "I used to see him in the gym, and his eyes—I've never seen eyes so bright." A picture of Brian teeing off was etched into his gravestone, for he loved golf most of all. For Brian—quiet, kind, leukemia—we planted a flowering dogwood on the schoolgrounds, in what had become a tradition.

In my sister's class, it was Chris Dobbins. The lazy summer day of Chris's accident, my sister and I followed the sound of a helicopter to the intersection of Route 30 and Wenger Road, where she recognized her classmate Danny's minivan. Danny had just gotten his license, and Chris had been in the passenger seat. We stood with the crowd and tried to interpret the gravity of the situation from Chris's mother's body language as she was escorted to the hospital.

"I think she looked okay," I offered.

"I think it took everything she had not to fall over," my sister said. She was right. Someone had been holding Mary up with every step she took toward her what awaited her.

Chris hadn't been a sports superstar—he was slight, a late bloomer—but he was well liked, a quintessential "good kid." As a community, we mourned his death as a tragedy, and another tree went into the ground.

In my brother's class, it was the third-grade teacher. Two days before Christmas in 1995, Toby Grim, the twenty-four-year-old son of a local car dealership owner and newly beloved elementary school teacher, was riding in a car with friends out doing some last-minute shopping. They hit an icy patch, went left of center into another vehicle, and Toby was killed. He had been a long-jumper—held the high school record—and in his memory, his parents donated money to replace the old cinder track with an all-weather surface and established a yearly relay event.

In 1999, Toby's older sister and mother opened a coffee shop too, something he'd talked about trying himself. Called the Bliss Café and serving classic espresso drinks none of us had ever heard of, it was the most cosmopolitan thing to ever appear on Main Street. The Bliss ran in the red for a decade, financed by car dealership money and raw memory, and then finally closed. The café had been a dream space—there were sandwiches named after Toby's toddlerisms and pictures of him hanging on the wall. For a wealthy family in a small town like ours, is fourteen years too long to justify investing in a dead man's dream? What, I wonder, are the economics of grief?

•••••••

The same year Chris Dobbins died, a sophomore named Becky Shubert also died in a car wreck, this time amid rumors of alcohol and truancy. The rumors were untrue—an article in the county paper, *The Daily Record*, specifies that "no alcohol was detected" and that Becky hadn't been at school on Monday because there had been no school that day. The crash was a rear-ending. The driver of the Cavalier in which Becky sat shotgun, a sixteen-year-old who'd had his license for exactly ten days, hit a pickup truck that had slowed as it crested a hill on Kidron Road. Slowing over a hill was a necessary precaution on Kidron Road, as it was a main thoroughfare for our Amish neighbors, and a horse and buggy could be clopping along unseen just over the horizon.

Two other passengers rode in the car with Becky, and they were seriously injured. Both were life-flighted and comatose, and Nicole, Becky's best friend, was treated in the burn unit. The reporting on the crash in our town paper, the *Gazette*, is detailed, almost gory. We learn that Nicole sustained facial injuries, that the "right side of her face was crushed . . . breaking all the bones," while the driver "suffered a broken thigh bone in his right leg." We read further that he "fractured three fingers in his left hand and needed 55 stitches in his right arm to close several cuts." Two unconscious bodies, compromised by disaster, leaked their secrets into the news.

Becky herself had recently gotten her license and indicated she wished to be an organ donor, for among the many freedoms we roared off with at sixteen was the choice, if we didn't come back, to reissue our strong and youthful hearts. So, Becky's corneas were removed and used to repair one small part of Nicole's shattered face.

Talk of money is also part of the article, which oddly mentions that Becky's parents did not carry a life insurance policy on her and that her father's employer had set up a memorial fund to offset funeral costs, a fund that had "already collected $1000." The driver's mother, in a heartbreakingly insufficient stay against the horror, notes that he had proper car insurance. A final telling detail also appears: "Rebecca J. Shubert of 110 N.W. Lebanon Road, Lot #70." That last bit, lot number 70, meant something to people reading the *Gazette*. Becky lived in the trailer park.

No tree was planted for Rebecca J. Shubert of 110 Northwest Lebanon Road, lot 70, and hardly anyone noticed. One brave voice took to the press, our junior high newspaper, and pointed out the hypocrisy: even here in our little podunk town, poor kids were nobodies. Becky wrote poetry, lines like "Life's a sculpture, friends are clay," which isn't even a bad conceit, but her only legacy is a cornea, staring back at all of us as we moved on and forgot her.

•••••••

The hill where Becky died overlooked the same intersection where I stalled the Saab into oncoming traffic, and two years after Mom got us out of third gear, I had my first crash there too.

The details fit the pattern. I was on my way to play a volleyball game. I looked to the right, up the hill; looked to the left, at the cheese shop and vet clinic; and then I turned right into a pickup truck. The truck was in my lane, having crossed over a double-yellow line in order to pass an Amish buggy coming down the same stretch of road the truck involved in Becky's crash had anticipated and lowered its speed for. A slight crunch, an abrupt stop. I got out, mortified despite not being at fault, and assessed the damage. The truck had not a scratch, while the Saab had a small dent in the hood and a cracked headlight (The headlights! They had wipers!). I was a teenager who was worried about being late, so when the man who had driven his enormous truck into my lane hopefully suggested there was nothing to report, I agreed and drove on to volleyball. My parents footed the repair bill.

•••••••

When I finally graduated high school and started college, my seven-minute daily commute over hilly chip-and-seal became occasional, uneventful two-hour trips up and down the wide, gently diagonal throughway of I-71. Meanwhile, back in my hometown, my cousin's sixteen-year-old sister-in-law entered Route 30 northbound, right in front of the Grim car dealership, and was killed by a semi that failed to brake at the bottom of a long grade. Janine's is the last fatal car accident in our town with which I'm familiar.

When Janine died, her story moved widely and with force. The truck had faulty brakes, which the driver had knowingly neglected, and he became only the second person in the state to be convicted of aggravated vehicular homicide based on an equipment violation. Janine had been active in her church and also played traveling softball, and both of these legacies appear in a passage about her life I later discovered in a devotional book called *Sister Freaks: Stories of Women Who Gave Up Everything for God,* written by Christian pop artist Rebecca St. James. "Even in death," the narrative reads, "Janine's passion for Christ changed lives." The essay ends by telling us that Janine's softball coach started regularly attending services at her church after her memorial.

The county newspaper also ran a piece about Janine a week after the accident. The article mentions the Christian youth organization Young Life and reports that a "7-foot cross . . . constructed by the high school's industrial arts class" was built for Janine and moved to her home church. The article quotes the student council treasurer: "Everybody's thinking about moving [the cross] to the school and putting it on display out front."

The cross is still at the church, according to my father, who told me he felt vaguely unnerved playing kickball beneath it.

•••••••

For several years, I lived near Omaha, and there, I noticed, kids died differently. In the city, with its lowered speed limits and grid system and interrupting stoplights, car wrecks took fewer lives than other high-speed projectiles.

At a local park in 2020, Waw W. Gach, eighteen years old, was shot in his head and killed. A Sudanese immigrant, Waw had attended high school in Iowa. I have searched for more details about his life, but all I can find is a second article that assures me, "18-year-old fatally shot at Benson Park was 'tremendous athlete.'"

The quotation comes from Waw's former football and track coach, who noted that while in high school, Waw played defensive back and "had one or two interceptions." In the high jump, though, Waw crossed an ocean to leap six feet, eight inches, leading the whole state of Iowa his junior season. "He was just an energetic young man," Waw's coach said, "and when you got to know him you found out that he had a tremendous personality. . . . He was full of energy and full of life."

• • • • • • •

Sometimes when I think about Mark Kiper and Sara Cottrell and Brian Slates and Chris Dobbins and Toby Grim and Becky Shubert and Janine Ramer and Waw Gach, I imagine the measure of my teenage life in a memorial plaque sound bite that never had to be written. I think about how in the newspaper, my varsity letters would have been tallied up and offered for consideration alongside my 4.0 GPA and the number of schoolmates who had counted me as their friend, concrete data points suggesting the shape and weight of my loss to a little Ohio community that most demonstrably mourned the physically gifted. So when I see that Waw Gach once leapt six feet, eight inches, in the state of Iowa, I am both saddened and relieved to know the exact size of our failure to understand his loss.

I have now lived somewhere other than small-town Ohio longer than I lived there, but when I consider the memorials we built and the memorials we didn't, I finally understand what is correct about the choice of the big, ugly cross: a child has died, and the cross is unseemly, like grief.

SONG AND DANCE MEN, PART I

I met Adam for the second time while he was walking barefoot through our mutual friend's wedding reception. He was twenty-two, and the shoes he'd worn to the ceremony were borrowed. He took them off because they pinched his toes.

At a party after the wedding, in a ravine where he'd built forts and a zipline, he got high and told me he thought he had a mouth fetish.

"You mean oral fixation?"

"That's the one."

His tongue was pierced.

A few days later, I had my first boyfriend, he had his first girlfriend, and they were us, and he introduced me to marijuana and trip-hop.

I drove Adam everywhere because he had recently been drunk behind the wheel. Before I found us jobs counting bugs for the state of Ohio, we hung drywall in his parents' basement. He sang while we screwed drywall into studs and then while we dropped grubs into petri dishes. He knew the lyrics to every song I had ever heard, and at parties he danced so fluidly you would never guess we'd first met while attending a local Mennonite high school where dancing was forbidden. His hair was blond, almost white, and it stood naturally in a kind of geometric 'fro, product free, his charm electric.

Adam and I still lived with our parents, and our friend Joas, who was a few years older, lived on our parents' couches. Joas was in and out of bands and work, so we passed him around our circle of friends like we were in a ten-headed custody battle. Straw-haired and wiry with a god's jaw line, he was a constant presence that summer, a traveling magnet we were proud to draw. Together, Adam and Joas sang at coffee shops and parties, legitimately and effortlessly talented. At shows, as the girlfriend, I was unsure how to sit and watch, feeling vaguely as though the pure beam of my affection might break something.

Joas wrote songs, made art, and gave tattoos without a license, sometimes in my bedroom. He charged whatever we felt like paying. In exchange for a Volvo with 266,666 miles on its stalled odometer, which broke down a week after he started driving it, Joas tattooed a Polish eagle onto my dad's calf but forgot the tail.

Our other friends were mostly men, mostly from home. There was Sam and Jon and Nate and Nathan and Devin and Alex and Ben. Many of them were a special kind of pot-smoking, peace-and-justice-loving liberal Mennonite you can find in only a few places on Earth, and one of those places happened to be where we'd all grown up. Among the group were multiple sets of cousins and brothers and a remarkable amount of goodwill. We drank and we smoked and we drank and we smoked, and we worked a little and laughed.

Near the end of the summer, Adam, Sam, and I went to a national park to eat mushrooms. Sam, who between his hairstyle, facial grooming, and outfit was usually making at least two statements, had been a child art prodigy, drawing photographic portraits at six. When the mushrooms took hold, I couldn't catch my breath for laughing at the clouds, but Sam wandered off. When he came back hours later, he told us a dragon had come out of the sky to have a heart-to-heart about his drinking—lately he'd taken to driving everywhere with an open beer can. His long brown curls were flecked with leaves, and he proclaimed he would paint more.

• • • • • • •

Summer ended, as it had to. I moved back to central Ohio to finish my last year of undergrad, Adam moved to a Mennonite enclave in Harrisonburg, Virginia, and we mostly lost touch. Occasionally I'd send him five dollars for a CD he sang on, and once, he emailed to ask about poetry. Eventually Joas bummed a ride to Harrisonburg so he could play drums in Adam's band. They lived next to mountains and made music together. Miraculously, no one fathered any children.

Meanwhile, I grew out of my parents' insurance coverage and as a graduate student watched my bank account hover around zero. Unlike my free and easy friends singing songs in the mountains, I worried about my finances. By about year four of graduate school, I also started to feel like my real life was just out of reach, that it lay somewhere at the end of the double rainbow of advanced degrees I was getting, though what that life would look like, I had no idea. I started to take out loans to travel, buy new clothes—anything that felt like living in the now.

Sam moved down to Virginia too. Most of the lovely boys from that summer were there now, living their young lives surrounded by pretty hippies with dreadlocks and no bras. Sam wasn't painting more often, though he was drinking as much. One weekend Adam and Sam went on a camping trip, where doubtless Adam shimmied up flexible saplings until the trees bowed him back to earth, something I'd watched him do when we went camping. But the only story I heard from this trip was that Adam had nearly cut off Sam's hand while they were play-fighting with sticks and machetes.

When the ambulance arrived, Sam stood with his arms up, his good hand clamped against his wrist.

"Have you been drinking?" the paramedics asked as they hustled toward him.

"What do you think?"

•••••••

When they hit their thirties, they all came home, Adam and Sam after traveling and working sporadically until they finally ran out of money living on a boat in Hawaii. Joas came back with a ponderous gut. Adam was losing his marvelous hair.

Adam and Joas both moved in with their parents, worked odd jobs under the table, and continued to perform together for next to nothing at coffee shops and bars. I took a weekend trip home from school to see them, and we visited the old drinking haunts. Adam rolled cigarettes while I chided him about health insurance.

When we left the bar and went back to our friends' house, we were shocked to find that not one of us had pot. While Joas and Adam were singing and playing guitar in the back room, the friends who were hosting—a set of brothers who were now in nursing school—asked what my sleeping plans were. I had cut myself off early in the evening and told them I planned to drive back to my dad's house that night. Ah, they said. We will have Joas for a while then.

Later, in the kitchen, the older of the brothers was talking diets with Joas, who flexed and requested that his biceps be assessed.

"Hey, man, I do push-ups every day," Joas said, and the brother showed him bags of spinach.

•••••••

When I turned thirty, I called Adam, who, like me, was still usually single, and returned home to host a party in an unoccupied house my dad was trying to sell. I was on winter break and looking forward to seeing lots of friends from home, but only four people made it. Sam was back in Hawaii. Joas finally, inevitably, had a kid on the way and was trying to party less. The last time he'd gone out, he was found stumbling in the direction of his truck saying he was an important man with important things to do in the morning. Adam took his keys, and Joas clocked him. Before I knew him, Joas and a few of our friends spent six months abroad at a tiny German Bible school tucked away at the foot of the Alps. One night, the brother who would later offer Joas spinach snuck out and then attempted to sneak back in through a window after curfew. He was caught by Joas, who meted out God's justice—a smack across the face—dressed in a bathrobe and sucking on a pipe.

On the night of my thirtieth birthday party in the abandoned house, Adam was the first to arrive, toothpick affixed in the corner of his mouth. He'd brought a folding chair, as I requested, since there was no furniture, and he immediately dragged it under the beeping smoke detector and changed out the old batteries with the new ones that were lying on the floor. As the other guests arrived, I noticed that Adam was talking nonstop, even more than usual, and playing techno nobody wanted to hear. Clearly, he was on something.

Apart from Adam's energy, the evening rolled on tamely, a sedentary night of talk. We were all getting older, but my gatherings had always been subdued. At the raucous house parties of our youth, I was the one worrying about noise violations, and sometimes my reflexive sharpness sliced through the miasma in ways that were decidedly not chill. During one of the first parties Adam and I attended together, we sat in the backyard in a circle of people on the ground. Someone accidentally knocked over a beer, and almost before it landed, I shot a reprimand at the offender. I don't remember what I said, only that it was both harsh and completely unnecessary. Everyone turned slowly to look at me: *What's up with her?*

By my thirtieth birthday, I still hadn't puzzled out their silent question. When finally I did, half a decade later, it was with a kind of wry shock that I realized two things: first, that I had long conflated two distinct states of being, and second, that in the process, I had fundamentally misunderstood my own personality, my periods of heavy idleness. *Oh,* I thought on that day. *Being depressed and being relaxed are not the same thing.*

My party meandered toward its close, and soon it was late. Everyone had gone home but Adam. We stepped out to have one last cigarette before retiring to our sleeping bags, and when I reached for the door, the knob wouldn't turn.

Oh, shit.

My dad had asked me to lock the door from the inside, so I did. He also warned me that the inside knob turned with the lock still in place, but I forgot. My dad's keys were now inside the house, and the only spare was secured in the realtor's lockbox. It was 2:00 a.m. on December 21, and while it was unseasonably warm, it had just started pouring rain, and I was drunk with no shoes on. Through the door's glass window, we could see, like a tiny asphalt pit, a bowl and a bag of weed lying together in the center of the living room carpet beside Adam's phone. I had my phone, and Adam had his keys.

We ran out to his truck, me barefoot, and tried to come up with a plan. We decided we'd sober up for a while and then drive to his parents' house thirty-five minutes away. The rain pattered on the windshield while we made superficial conversation in a purgatorial state of sobriety. Eventually, Adam decided he could drive, and we headed out. "It's weird being your passenger for once," I observed.

I worried he was not as sober as he said he was, that he'd get pulled over again, or worse, and this time it would be my fault. But we got to his parents' house fine, and he quietly showed me some of the remodeling work he'd recently completed. Always good at residential construction, he had assembled enough odd jobs over the years to become a skilled craftsman. His bedroom was in the basement, so we went down. We lay beside one another, and his pleasure was cartoonish.

Sometimes when we first knew each other, Adam and I would get so high, we couldn't even manage sex. Our hands would find each other's bodies, and we'd soon discover all we could handle was lying in each other's arms. "I want to have sex," he'd sigh. "But it's just too much." And I'd go back to rubbing his back or running my fingers through his hair and feeling intensely, pleasurably overfull at even this touch.

That night, I was not where he was and couldn't help but laugh at him. It finally came out that he had snorted something he found in an old jacket before the party, probably an analog of Molly, he thought. His bed was screwed into the wall, and I was anxious about all the creaking, and he had only one old condom, and it broke. So we stopped and went to sleep.

• • • • • • •

In the morning, I refused to go upstairs until I was sure Adam's parents had gone out. The issue wasn't that I didn't like them—I did. I was just embarrassed. I was thirty years old, and I'd sneaked into the basement of their home with their thirty-one-year-old son and tried and failed to have quiet sex on an extremely loud bed.

After the locked-up house keys had been sorted, Adam and I arranged to meet again for supper so that I could return his belongings—but also to talk, since we'd never gotten around to catching up that whole stupid night. He arrived in his work clothes, khaki pants and a black fleece vest over Under Armour. He was reflooring the offices of the factory where he worked and told me he was in line to take over as plant supervisor. "In the winter, when it's cold, we make the airstrip sealant. In the summer and fall, we travel in crews and apply it to the runways," he explained.

Though Adam was shorter than me by a few inches, he was cut and compact, with a clarion voice I had loved deeply for the way it hummed in his bristly chest, resonating through his torso and head and into my ear. While I thought fondly of those times, the conversation hopped sporadically from topic to topic until it became clear that neither of us would be ordering a second drink. Somehow we'd gotten onto the topic of vaccination, and in the crosshairs of his booming voice and my flat one, pissed each other off.

When we had re-met after high school, he was still thoroughly Mennonite, a pacifist, and once, when we argued about my atheism and I told him I found his offer to pray for me insulting, he cried. In the intervening years, I had continued along my path, shooting high and straight through the world of traditional knowledges, while he meandered among conspiracies and vapid stoner talk. Now, over a burger, he expressed doubts about vaccines, told me he had gone apocalyptic and bought a gun. It only seemed fair, I replied, that he give up Jesus in exchange, as he'd just forfeited the only admirable thing about Christianity. He laughed.

That night, after I bought Adam's supper as an apology and said goodbye, I thought about my tenuous relationships with the free-spirited, the rhetorical gaffes that had always given me away as punctual and rule oriented in their company. Once, while at a party with Sam, everyone was on acid but me. He'd invited me to the party after I canceled my own on account of snow. We had never texted each other before, but in our back-and-forth, my place was immediately reestablished. I told him he should invite his brother, which led to this conversation:

> S: My unhappily married brother? My happily married brother? Or my happily unmarried brother?
>
> E: Jon. I've seen him more than you in the last few years
>
> S: First of all, no you haven't because I see Jon daily at work
>
> E: I mean I have seen him more times than I've seen you doofus

Of course Sam understood what I meant and was just pretending not to because I was very easy to prod. At the periphery of the imaginative spaces my friends moved through, I often stood pointing. Sometimes I poked holes in their delicate suspensions of reality, which before my clarifying impulse had been hanging like glittering, transient bubbles in the conversational ether. Other times, I belabored jokes by explaining precisely how funny they'd been. Because of these habits of mind, I'd always walked among them as the overly educated, extremely gullible one. When after high school I reintroduced myself to the brothers who would become nurses in a garage lined with plastic lawn chairs and beer coolers, I informed them that I went by Elizabeth now, as the merging of the *z*'s in Liz Zaleski had started to drive me crazy. The younger brother, Alex, looked at me seriously and asked, "Your name's not Lisa Leski?" In response to my stunned silence, he broke into a laugh, mercifully letting me in on the joke. Not two minutes later, we were talking about his stepbrother, and I asked what he looked like to make sure I was remembering the right person. "Well, pretty generic. He's got two eyes, two ears . . ."

"Two arms," I jumped in, eager to show I could play along.

Alex looked grave. "Well, before the accident."

Oh, Christ!

And on and on it went, the playful troupe two steps ahead and me jogging behind, insisting, "Hey, I'm smart, I promise!"

At the party with Sam, to which I wore a holey T-shirt, I had a few beers and held a pet snake. Sam looked quintessentially like Sam, which is to say very rad. He had pulled the long hair around the crown of his head into a wavy ponytail, but the rest of his head was shaved, and he sported a pinstripe coat with sheepskin lapels, a tie-dye shirt, and sunglasses, indoors. We hadn't seen each other in a long time, and even though he was tripping and I was not, we were basically on the same page, we paid attention to each other, and a few days later, he even followed up on a conversation we'd had about cults: "By the way, I'm starting an agnostic commune where I'm the leader please bring your children."

At some point in the evening, though, I noticed another man at the party had an incredible mane of hair, and I made the mistake of trying to listen to him. He stood in front of the dining room table, from which position he warned us of a small group of powerful, nefarious intellectual elites. This cabal of scholars, he said, was responsible for the direct suppression of grassroots epiphanic knowledge of the sort he was then laying down. "College is a conspiracy," he proclaimed.

He was the one on LSD, but as he flew off, I felt the same kind of bottoming out that accompanies drug paranoia, a fearful awareness of the gap that has opened up between your conscious reality and that of others in the room. He raced along on his delusion, misusing theoretical jargon and attributing an enviable amount of power to university professors. A cog in the machine, a flunky for the man, a vibe harsher and pedant who had never learned to leave well enough alone, I barged into his fantasy with the realities of academic work.

Gah, I'd blown my cover. Not only was I not on acid, but I'd also gone to college for a very long time!

I typed out notes about our conversation on my phone in the half-assembled basement bathroom. I also wrote in all caps that the state of this bathroom was UNACCEPTABLE. Who were these people still living this life, of summer, of youth, of scraping and sponging?

After my frustrating supper with Adam, I imagined future parties in which I choked down cigarettes to cover the scent of my good credit score while Adam snorted something he serendipitously came upon. For him, the promise of the future would always seem an arm's reach away, fat and ripe with possibility, even when it wasn't. And for me, the promise would never quite arrive, always staved off by my preparations for it.

•••••••

I continued jumping through my highly structured hoops while the beautiful boys from home invented occupations for themselves. Devin made yarn in a barn. Nate, one of the brother nurses told me, just kept being Nate until he bumbled into a nice house and a good job purely on account of being himself. The last time I talked to Adam, who'd sloshed himself into a second driving suspension, I asked him what Joas was up to, and he told me he'd gotten into knife making. "You know," Adam said. "Joas shit."

I believe it was the same brother nurse, Alex, who a few years ago broke the news that Adam was "laying low" back in Virginia, off grid, avoiding federal investigators. I'd already "finished" this essay and hadn't been in touch with Adam since. One of the many risks of perfectionism, I continue to learn, is how the world careens on past your careful work, leaving behind not just the events but your understanding of them. Another decade will probably pass before I figure out what to say in response to the news reports showing

Adam, wearing a mustache and a polka-dot cowboy hat, walking the halls of the Capitol on January 6, 2021.

All I can say for sure is that I prefer the old ending to this essay, which was written in a world preceding the last paragraph's events and so skipped right over them to this:

When I returned to school at the end of that golden summer, before Adam moved down to Virginia, he was left without a ride to our bug job. He fixed up an old scooter and buzzed in and out until winter. Years later, when the supervisory position at the factory fell through because he'd lost his license again, Adam went back to working word-of-mouth contractor gigs—flooring, framing, setting tile. To get to the job sites, he rigged up a bicycle trailer and pedaled his tools to and fro.

In the decade that had passed between that first improvised transport and the second, little changed in the two of us—we had not grown apart, only deeper into ourselves. As now, in this moment, when instead of occupying the present, I am squeezing the unstated, unbound joy of the past into an overt shape, expounding on the meaning, just in case anyone missed it. For instance: I've often thought it poetic that my first love was named Adam. First man, garden dweller, eternal child of God.

HYMN

Once, while standing near the front of 250 schoolmates and teachers all singing "Open the Eyes of My Heart, Lord," I placed an orange construction cone on top of my head and began hopping up and down. I'd just offered the eyes of my heart to God for dilation, but the eyes in my head saw nothing but an orange haze. I clapped my hands and tossed my arms up and down, rocking forward in fits of laughter.

The singers surrounding me were Mennonite, so they knew whatever was going on with me over there in seat 34B had nothing to do with God—the Mennonite God was too well-mannered to incite holy convulsions. To be sure, my cone dance was not an act of worship, but it was the single most transcendent experience of my life.

I was laughing with abandon, my breath warming and dampening the air around my head, my voice buzzing flatly off the rubbery walls. Cut off from the visual of the crowd, I imagined an empty space expanding around me until I was the only one standing in the room, hopping in place, the cone flopping from side to side. I still can't adequately explain why this was the happiest moment of my life, but for the fifteen seconds I passed flailing in front of a crowd, blind to everything but my own joy, I was more myself than I ever had been or ever would be again. I was eighteen years old.

The orange construction cone had presented itself to me that afternoon as I walked into the Performing Arts Center for chapel, as I did every weekday for a half hour of songs, prayers, skits, and speeches. A cluster of seats was under repair along the far aisle, and the pylon marked their sequestering. I saw the cone and felt a calling as to a vocation. "Ah," I thought. "*There's* the cone I'm supposed to put on my head during the praise song."

Normally, this would be the part of the story where I told you I was suffering. That I was stuck in a tyrannical religious school and had frolicked defiantly, in a spirit of resistance and self-liberation. That after this moment, I broke from the repressive mores of my community and discovered a friendlier version of God, one who joined me in giving a thumbs-up to asylum seekers and a thumbs-down to ICE. But that's not the story. Not at all. It's true though, that like the kids in *Footloose,* we weren't allowed to dance.

My enrollment in a Mennonite high school had nothing to do with religion or even education. My family wasn't Mennonite, though we couldn't rightly call ourselves Catholic anymore, as we'd stopped going to mass when I was twelve, and the small public school I'd been attending for elementary and junior high was comparable, if not slightly better academically, than Central Christian. No, I attended one of the only Mennonite-run high schools in the country because I played softball very well.

The nineties were the golden age of American women's fastpitch, and my sister and I played on nationally competitive traveling teams. All summer long, Erin struck out future NCAA champs as one of the best fifteen-year-old pitchers in the world. Our local public high school team, however, was a sorry affair, and at the helm was one of my many uncles. For reasons both valid and petty, my parents lobbied for his firing. This debacle exploded our extended family, and after eighth grade, when it came time for me to wade into the rank small-town politics that had been seething since, my parents pulled the drain and sent both my sister and me down the road to Central.

We knew the softball coach at Central, and though our new team also happened to be better than my uncle's, the goal of our transfer had been simple: to place us elsewhere. In fact, the preeminent sport at our new school was volleyball, and the first time I met any of my classmates was at volleyball camp the summer before my freshman year. In the hours of drilling inside the blue-padded brick walls of Gym 2, I soon found that Mennonites play volleyball with a skill and intensity that belies their meek worldview, though in other ways, this passion dovetails gracefully. For its violence, the sacred American pastime of football was eschewed, and instead, we worshipped at the divide of the volleyball net. In our kneepads and ankle braces, we dove and leapt with a contained aggression, each team on their own side, a bouncy ball mediating contact.

Between wall sits and hitting lines, I started to meet my peers, a hardworking and even-keeled set of Bethanys and Rebeccas with a high percentage of shared last names: Miller, Steiner, Troyer, Weaver, Nussbaum. Slavic -skis were an anomaly, and when my new class of forty-six arranged ourselves alphabetically on the first day of school, I usurped last place from Mark Yoder, who had tried to genially halt me as I marched past him to the ultimate seat in the final row. At volleyball camp, the day had been broken into two sessions, and we ate lunch together in the cafeteria, where instead of discrete tables, long rows of joined benches created a communal effect. I sat beside Bethany and watched her dissect an artichoke, a vegetable I had never seen in its whole form, and dip its hearts into butter.

Once the school year was officially underway, I sat attentively in chapel and began to further orient myself. When I started high school, I no longer considered myself Catholic, but I was certainly a Christian, and for the previous year or two, I had been attending a Protestant church with my maternal grandparents. At school, I learned that Mennonites identify as Anabaptists, a term that means "rebaptize" and encompasses the Amish and Hutterites as well, and that they refer to their faith as a "third way," a set of beliefs that is neither Protestant nor Catholic. The flavor of Anabaptism that defined the school was fairly liberal and deeply pacifistic. This was not lip-service pacifism but a historic, practical, and principled legacy. While my grandfathers had both been drafted into the military, one leaving the farm to serve in World War II and the other, who had started but abandoned seminary, serving in the Korean War, the family histories of my schoolmates and teachers were full of men who had been consigned to work camps as conscientious objectors.

Most of my friends could trace their ancestors back to small clusters of Swiss-German immigrants who had fled persecution and martyrdom in Europe. For a field trip, we once rode twenty minutes south to visit *Behalt*, a 2,650-square-foot cycloramic mural depicting Anabaptist history. *Behalt* means "to remember," and the artwork has been dubbed the "Sistine Chapel of the Amish and Mennonites." Indeed, the audacious colors and dark tenor of many of the painting's scenes were more akin to the stations of the cross and stained-glass abjection I'd grown up with than the bright, clean, unostentatious aesthetic I'd come to expect of Mennonite spaces. There, on the subtly curving wall, alongside the buggies and windmills of the peaceful periods, a shirtless man stood tied to a post, tongues of fire consuming his shins.

Mennonites wore their inherited martyrdom with uncharacteristic pride, and in my church history class, I learned about Menno Simons, their namesake founding father, as well as the *Martyrs Mirror*, an enormous, gory volume from the seventeenth century that details the sufferings of early Christians in part 1 and Anabaptists specifically in part 2. Interspersed with the testimonies of the persecuted, over a hundred copper etchings appear with such matter-of-fact captions as "Blandine half-roasted on a grill and then thrown to wild bulls, AD 172."

Anabaptism's pacifist doctrine and uneasy history with institutional power meant that we didn't hang a flag at school or sing the national anthem before sporting events. Our mascot Bluester was a rotund teddy bear who circled the concession stand doling out hugs while the volleyball team—dressed in bright, roomy athletic shorts instead of spandex—demolished schools three times our size. Our stiffest competition was another, even smaller Mennonite school two hours southwest, Shekinah Christian, whose players wore mid-calf white skorts. Their middle hitter, a young woman who clipped a partial head covering into her blond braid and probably never got a bachelor's degree, could have gone on to play for a Division I college. After we'd squared off in our dowdy threads, regardless of whether they won or lost, Shekinah gathered in a circle on the court, put their hands in, and shouted, "Praise the Lord!"

Once, after high school, at a Mennonite picnic dominated by sects more conservative than the congregations that ran my school, I watched the volleyball net go up and women in bonnets and dresses play the most hardcore recreational volleyball I've ever seen.

No one at my school wore a bonnet or the plain-cut monochrome dresses some of the girls at my public school had worn. The more traditional Mennonite branches venerated extreme frugality and set little store by education, so despite the fact that the tuition was comparatively cheap for a private school (it was $4,000 a year for me, and most Mennonite students received aid from their congregations that reduced their tuition significantly), the most visible Mennonites in our community did not attend.

In most ways, our curriculum was standard. I learned evolution and had just one extra religion class required per year. In one of those classes, I remember arguing with the teacher about his metaphorical reading of Christ's infamous "camel through the eye of a needle" analogy. He suggested an alternate reading wherein one must simply hold the eye of the needle up to one's *own* eye, after which the tiny gap appears to take in a generous swath of applicants, including the rich. "This passage," he said, "is about perspective." Aside from the fact that a needle's eye cannot in any way be arranged as a monocle—I immediately went home and tried it—I thought this a self-serving interpretation and preferred the literal version.

After all, I was aware that several of my schoolmates were the children or grandchildren of millionaires, families who owned their own businesses, usually in home building, manufacturing, or insurance. And though displays of wealth were anathema, wealth was not. It came as no surprise to me that Eastern Mennonite University offered an invented master's program in something called "conflict transformation" alongside a regular old MBA. College felt noncompulsory for many of my peers, who had immediate pathways to steady work in a family business. I'd been lucky to get a job at one of these businesses the summer before my senior year so I could help pay my tuition. The monthly checks had become a burden on my mother, and she was considering sending me back to my old school.

The business was a woodshop that sold mostly home décor, and I spent the day either sanding or wiping wood stain into the carved veneers of medium-density fiberboard. We had a laser cutter that burned entire hymns into rectangles the height and width of a hymnal. I ran my sander over "Come, Thou Fount of Every Blessing," removing the light burn marks the laser had left while carving the staves and lyrics.

In addition to high school kids, the woodshop employed a number of Holdeman Mennonite teens who worked full-time. I had never met anyone from this particular sect, and when we were at the staining station and had our earplugs out, I chatted away with Roxie and Audrey, who wore black head coverings but dresses in bright patterns. As Holdeman women, they had stopped attending school at sixteen and were not allowed to pursue further education except to become a nurse or a teacher. The community's most surprising restriction was on music: instruments were banned from their churches and radios from their cars, the human voice the only sound permitted in worship.

Music, particularly the singing of hymns, was the other mainstay of our school. Mennonites are masters of four-part harmony, and though the administration didn't support cutting players from varsity sports teams, the choirs were systematically rid of their baggage. Indeed, the select nature of the top sixteen-person choral ensemble, a group we actually called "varsity singers," lent it as much social capital as the volleyball team.

I was a decent musician who knew music theory and played a few instruments, but I sang poorly and was cut from mere concert choir my junior year. The tryouts were held the week before Christmas break, the lists posted in January. My friends and I were so eager to know our fate, we pursued the choir director, Tim (in a commitment to radical equality, students called teachers by their first names), into the music room after our Christmas assembly and asked for the verdict.

"You just want a thumbs-up or thumbs-down?" he asked, standing by the shelves of sheet music.

We nodded.

He grimaced slightly and gave Laura and me a thumbs-down. Becca, who was one of the few students destined for a nonreligious college, the Manhattan School of Music, got a thumbs-up. Thirteen years later, I saw Tim at a funeral for another former teacher, and he told me he still remembered the discomfort of this moment. At the funeral, the hymns faltered in my throat, my voice thick with sorrow.

Our Christmas breaks rolled into a two-week service learning experience called "mini-term," and the offerings ranged from auctioneering to animal husbandry to studying human rights issues along the United States–Mexico border. Certain mini-terms were held in the summer, so anyone taking a summer-break session had an extra two-week vacation to start the year. The opportunities were diverse and imaginative, and inevitably, some went better than others. Our freshman and sophomore English teacher was a mild-mannered man named Gabe, and after a string of optimistic mini-term expeditions ended in disaster, he left teaching altogether and quietly returned to cabinetmaking. In his bird-watching course, he sensed he had failed to inspire, the quiet majesty of ornithological discovery eluding his students until one afternoon, at a marsh, he heard Derrick exclaim, "Would you look at that?" Gabe turned and scanned the water, his heart suspended—a great blue heron? a swan? "Somebody threw a *TV* in there!"

My sister took part in another of Gabe's mini-terms, a summer bicycling tour of Ohio. The students trained in the weeks leading up to the trip, yet at the close of each day, they found themselves sprawled on the ground, exhausted but still somehow shy of their destination. They camped in a state park, where their supplies were beset by raccoons, and in their desperate final hours, they took to the highway in an attempt to make up time. The whine of a siren pursued them until, at the next exit, they were escorted off the freeway by state patrol. Gabe went home and stared at his map. What had gone wrong? And then he saw it—the hatched scale at the bottom of our heart-shaped state. His carefully plotted fifty-kilometer intervals had been fifty miles apiece. I imagine after that, his cabinet doors were measured not just twice but three times.

My senior year, I took the border issues course, which began with a reeking twenty-hour van ride with nine other high schoolers; crossed into Agua Prieta, Mexico, to hear from workers' rights organizers at *maquiladoras*; and ended at a US Border Patrol facility, where we watched a migrant be arrested via long-distance camera feed. I had noticed T-shirts for sale when we entered the building, which read, "You haven't truly hunted until you've hunted man." The border patrol agents laughed loudly when the man was caught.

I stood in the back of the room, watching the screen. I had seen the man jump in surprise when the border agent reached him, and it was this subtle movement, of shock and disappointment in the barren expanse of desert, that caused the agents to laugh. An indignation rose up in me—this, I thought, was the callous disregard Christ called on us all to bear witness to, to testify against.

"Why are you laughing?" I said, just as loudly as they had laughed. "There's nothing funny about it."

The agents quieted and did not respond—the tour was over. My fellow high schoolers found my outburst excruciating, and I could hear the boys complaining about it through the walls of our adjoined bedrooms at night. But if you had been paying attention in class and chapel, as I had, if you truly believed it was your responsibility to condemn violence in all its forms, as I did, it seemed impossible not to have said something.

I'd had no plans to make a scene at the border, and as I rehashed the moment again and again, I thought about my three and a half years at Central and how I had come to occupy such a position with such moral certitude. What was I anyway? I didn't call myself Mennonite, because I hadn't grown up in a Mennonite family, and in our region, the tradition was so strong, it bordered on an ethnicity. Truth be told, I had burgeoning doubts about divinity, but the compelling question seemed one less of faith than of fidelity. Despite having been immersed in the finer points of three different forms of Christianity—Catholicism, evangelical Protestantism, and Anabaptism—I found that the message of Christ was not especially difficult to interpret. Were you practicing unequivocal compassion and nonviolence? If not, then you were doing Christianity wrong.

I believed this wholeheartedly, and yet, in a moment that might have sealed me peaceably to these values, I seemed to have overreached and tipped into belligerence. Even in disagreement, God's limitless *agape* love—not antagonism—was the ideal. I'd done the right thing, I decided, but should have been nicer about it.

We were godly people but not gods, and one of the ways the school itself fell short of its ideals was in its uneven application of leniency. When a board member's child or a varsity singer was caught breaking the behavioral contract we signed—known as the "covenant"—they weathered the fallout from their lake party drinking bash more smoothly than the "troubled" kids sent to us by their parents as a last resort, who, along with pregnant girls, had a tendency to simply disappear. Once, though, the stars of the spring musical were kicked off the production for minor infractions, and as we braced the efforts of the second string, we wondered if perhaps there had been a miscalculation, whether the true punishment hadn't fallen on the audience.

Sometimes, too, the gentle and trusting moral oversight of the adults in our lives contracted into a *Dateline*-special hysteria. The most memorable of these spasms followed a visit from a man who had worked tangentially with big acts in the music industry, a fact that granted him formidable powers of ethical discernment. He was introduced by Miriam, our religion teacher, who had grown up Amish and instead of "yeah" still chanted a musical "ja, ja, ja" in the affirmative. In her green khakis, she stood at the podium and phonetically butchered Metallica, Megadeth, and Eminem. Then our guest speaker rose and ruined all our fun.

The notion of evil was not one that preoccupied us, and in truth, we hardly thought of souls. Mostly, we talked about love and peace and faith. If there was any spoon-feeding of ideology, that ideology was "Be kind to and serve other human beings." Now we were being asked to consider how near to Satan we were being led by Marilyn Manson. Our visitor's claims riled us into such a panic, we reconvened for a second emergency chapel while he was still on campus. And instead of posing thoughtful questions about the nature of censorship, the role of metaphor in art, or the intersection of aesthetics and ethics, we raised our hands one by one and offered the names of our favorite bands as chaff for his unquenchable fire.

"Amy Grant? Didn't she get a divorce?"

A week of hysteria followed, in which the conversation drifted home and my friends' parents scratched up and threw away CDs. Gradually, though, the stench of brimstone faded until we found ourselves back where we had started, singing our hymns and praying for one another's trivial concerns. In hindsight, the stricter aspects of school weighed heavier on my Mennonite friends—who were always surrounded, sometimes buoyantly and sometimes claustrophobically, by family, church, and community—than me. I could dip in at school and then leave, eating supper under different customs than lunch. For heaven's sake, my parents were Metallica fans, and when I came home from our perfunctory sex ed course, Mom and Dad were there to tell me more than I could ever want to know.

Despite the superficial sex ed, the strapless dress proscriptions, and our avoidance of spandex, I insist: we did not live in a culture of bodily shame. After gym class, we were required to shower, and most of us girls rinsed in the big, open stalls of the Gym 1 locker room. I can still remember the shapes of my friends' breasts, how we laughed together at mine (four cup sizes hence, my right breast still lags far behind my left). Not everyone appreciated the fact that we had to shed our clothes after gym, and sometimes when I tell other people about our communal bathing, they cringe, remembering their own insecurity. But I am thankful for the implicit lesson of our nakedness, the confirmation that underneath, we were all just variations on a theme.

That I could feel so comfortable in my teenage body was due partly to my parents and partly to the benevolent modesty of my teachers and peers. At age fourteen, when I went to one very particular high school instead of another, I diverged from several learning curves, chief among them the study of feminine adornment. In my old school, the most sought-after distinction for girls, even smart, accomplished girls like me, was to be thought pretty by boys. At Kelly's birthday party in seventh grade, we first listened to the Spice Girls and then to our friend Ashley, who sat in the crammed living room and matched grooming tools to our imperfections. "You," she said to a future salutatorian, "need a blackhead extractor." At my new school, in the relaxed and bare-faced complexions of my new friends, I saw the only invitation I needed to renounce my blow dryer. Now in the mornings, I slept in another fifteen minutes and let my hair dry naturally into waves. Two years later, on the first day of school my junior year, my efforts stopped at jeans and a T-shirt. In the hall, I passed my friend Carmen, a senior who in a typical high school culture might have looked down from the considerable height of her beauty and talent with a cutting gaze. "Wow, you really went all out for today, didn't you?" she said. Then she broke into a wide, bright smile and chuckled, "Man, I love you."

I am forty-one years old and cannot apply eye liner.

Thank god for the gift of this ignorance.

I didn't go on a single date in high school, and for that I am even more grateful. I still don't know how they managed it—surely, some credit is owed to the fact that half the school was related to each other—but somehow, the community built a space for us where dating felt optional. And while most of my best friends did have steady boyfriends or girlfriends our junior and senior years and some of them, of course, were having sex, at the heart of our connections to one another was something blessedly innocent, platonic, and true—as if, because we'd been given the chance to love ourselves, we did.

I lost my virginity at the age of twenty-one to someone who had been in my high school SALT group—a small, mixed-age affiliation that met once a month during chapel for group discussions, "sharing and learning together." At twenty-two, he was also still a virgin, and before we kissed, he sat in the glow of a bonfire and told me that some mornings in high school, he awakened from erotic dreams about me. Before his dream came true, our extended virginity was unremarkable, a common story in a world where sexuality was neither emphasized nor repressed.

On the other hand, a quarter of my class married itself within three years of graduating, at least partially for the sanctified sex. Even my sister married a Mennonite classmate at nineteen. Like many of her classmates' partnerships, hers dissolved two years later and was soon laughed off as a "starter marriage." In this way—and later, in my own doomed relationships with two Mennonite men who shared the same last name but no known relation—we fell away from the fold, remaining interlopers in a world we had belonged to but briefly.

Sometimes at school, I had the sense of being an interesting white person. A white person with a distinct culture and history that was not shared by the other white students, who outside our walls were the more obvious candidates for anthropological study. I felt this way, for instance, when I fielded theological questions about my former Catholicism in our Christian Family Living class. In this class, I negotiated ideals for disciplining children and sharing domestic labor as wife number 1 in an incidentally polygamous marriage with a pretend husband. There wasn't an even number of boys and girls in the room, and in 2001, Mennonites weren't talking about gay marriage yet. When shortly after graduating, a notable percentage of my sister's class came out, though, it was no surprise. We'd listened to our friends' stories about their former schools in other towns, some in other states, where they were called f—ts and feared violence. Some of our Black friends told similar stories, how they'd made a bargain for safety and opportunity. We were not a diverse school, though we were more diverse than my public school had been, and at times the sheltered whiteness that informed the curriculum frustrated them. But here, at least, Liz wouldn't have slurs whispered behind her back, and Noah had more options than he would at his inequitably funded, hard-knock public school. In the years following, as we found each other on social media, my friends' parents appeared smiling alongside their daughters' wives on Facebook, and the love of God survived. In the wake of George Floyd's murder, Beth asked us if we had ever *really* talked about race, about structural racism in America post–civil rights. No, we had not, we admitted. Gabe came out of hiding to say, *Thank you for asking this question*, and *I see now that we made it hard to be heard. I am very sorry about that.*

As I got closer to college, as I closed the wrinkled laminate of my Bible after reading it cover to cover a second time, I sometimes sensed that my heart was receding and my mind ascending. I asked more pointed questions and was less generous with my considerations. I scoffed at eternity and instigated debates that revealed the more strident tendencies I'd displayed in Arizona: I made a lot of noise over Psalm 149:3 and other pro-gyrating Bible verses, even though I had—and still have—no interest in social dancing. Doubt came earlier for me than my friends, who years after I had given it all up for good would send me updates, baby steps in their agnostic journeys: "Hey, how are you? I think Hell is a metaphor too."

I remember clearly the evening in college when, among a different type of Christian, my becoming finally became. I was sitting impatiently through a period of silence as my new friends bowed their hand-knitted hats and clasped their fingerless gloves, feeling out whether or not they were moved to speak. We met in a cluster of houses for nondenominational Bible studies, and I didn't yet have a name for the manner in which these people all looked and talked alike. When "hipster" reentered the lexicon, I pinned it beneath my memories of their God-as-cool-guy rhetoric, which grated on me as they addressed the omnipotent: "You're just so awesome, God. So *awesome*."

After the invocation, I listened one last time as a woman attempted to jam together the incompatible halves of the Old Testament and the New. I thought about my Bible teacher in high school doing the same, recalled the parable of the shrunken camel. At that moment, the teleology of Christianity appeared before me as an incongruous, jerry-rigged jigsaw. I found myself raising my hand, saying, "I'm sorry, but that just doesn't make any sense," and closing my own inquiry with a gavel.

I still have an old prayer journal, given to me by a youth pastor in junior high, and when I opened it recently, I was struck by the prophetic nature of her spelling mistake. We called these notebooks "Quiet Time" journals, and on the inside of the cover of mine, under Psalm 119:97b, "I meditate on your word all day long," she had written in elegant blue ink, "Your Quit Time Book."

Some time before I quit Christianity in college, and just before I stood before armed border guards and shouted at them for their lack of compassion in my senior year of high school, I took a class called Peace and Justice Issues with a new math teacher who clomped through the halls in tan, gently pointed wooden clogs. He spoke of his unconventional footwear as a sort of meditative practice, an opting out of hustle and bustle. In this class we held earnest and agonized debates about the limits of pacifism that sometimes devolved into questions about our hypothetical time-traveling obligation to kill Hitler, given the opportunity: "But what if you could just push a button and Hitler would die immediately and painlessly, and millions of people would be saved—you still wouldn't do it?" This teacher had recently graduated from Goshen, a very liberal Mennonite college in Indiana, and he was at the school only briefly before he moved to Virginia to work as a statistician for the US Census Bureau.

He was also my group's leader in the senior seminar, an intermittent lecture series meant to prepare us for life after high school, in which he read my increasingly snarky critiques of theological messages I found irrational. In one, I lambasted the notion of God "calling" anyone to do anything, particularly the businessman we'd just heard from who claimed he had followed such a call to great financial success. A few days later, he handed my essay back with his own two-page, single-spaced response. I no longer have my essay, but I still have his. He wrote that my complaint had been a “humorous, thoughtful, and provocative” piece that aimed to answer two age-old questions: “How do humans sense or understand the revelation of God?” and “How does one ‘know’ a decision or action represents the will of God?” He first defers: “It would be . . . presumptuous and arrogant to pretend I know the answer to such questions. In fact, my epistemology forbids me from making such truth claims.” And then he proceeds:

> Through a process of listening to silence, prayerful reflection, Biblical study, and dialogue (or polylogue) within the hermeneutical community, the “right” decision usually emerges. . . . The causes of [a] calling are complex and multifaceted, for they intersect with my environment, my persona, and various existential forces outside my small universe. . . . In response to the epistemic question regarding knowledge of God’s will, my comments are much shorter and concise. Might I suggest that one can never know the will of God?

I must have made some ambitious predictions about how my own life would turn out absent the call of God, because at one point, he politely questions the likelihood that I would be able to reconcile “logic” with “love and service.” In closing, he replies to an original statement lost to time: “I’m not entirely sure what people mean by having Jesus in their heart. The whole idea of possessing Jesus seems like an absurdity.”

He shuffled out to the softball field some evenings to watch us play. To watch me play, I think. At eighteen, the bones of my face had just finished growing into their shape, which was lovely and angular, and my skin glowed porelessly in complete defiance of adolescence. After the games, I took off my spikes and walked through the hallways in my dusty socks, stopping by my locker and peeking into the teacher's lounge, where often he sat facing a desktop computer, typing away. Sometimes I'd go in and we'd talk about morality, the two of us seated far from each other, our hands folded in our laps.

When I graduated, he wrote me a letter in which he thanked me for my frequent dissent, the critiques that kept him from complacency and boredom, but added, "I hope you will also continue to balance your criticism with affirmation and joy. I often feel tempted to enter an *uber*critical state, but have learned to find peace between criticism and compliance."

The next year in college, shortly after I left the nondenominational hipster house church never to return, a stranger approached me while I sat on a stone step, licking an ice cream cone, and asked if he could ask me a question. I said yes and then put my mouth back on my ice cream. He asked, "Do you believe in God?" And then we both watched as my ice cream scoop slid off the cone and splattered onto the sidewalk. "Ha!" I cried, the negative affirmation puddling into a sticky blue lake at our feet. "Not anymore."

I was adrift, but less because of anything to do with God than because I was also not with *them* anymore, with Bethany and Becca and Tim and Miriam, bending down to grab a hymnal on my way into chapel. I'd grown dismissive in my final days of high school, thinking I'd gotten the lesson and could replicate it on my own—in the far-flung biological field sites I saw in my future, here, at the second-largest university in America. My friends, for the most part, still had their community, just in new locales. I'd aimed rather "higher," and in my college application letters to the nation's top secular schools—schools where I was not accepted—I wrote with a combination of naivete, idealism, and hubris that now reads as slightly deranged. My sister had soldiered forward into community work in education and healthcare, seemingly immune to cynicism. But me—with my high school years bookended by Mennonite kindness and my undergraduate years now far removed from it—I'd left the flock confident in my ability to carry our radical love forward, while on my own, I seemed capable of affirming nothing.

One day I received a surprise package in my dorm room containing Tobias Wolff's *In the Garden of the North American Martyrs* with an inscription from the peace and justice teacher: "After waiting 1.5 years I finally bought a pair of tennis shoes. Perhaps clogs are for martyrs. For some reason, reading this book made me think of you." I read the book of short stories, and it drove the final nail into the coffin of my biology degree. Not only had I failed to reconcile logic with love, I didn't especially believe in logic either. Instead, I seemed destined for unceasing criticism—that ubercritical state I'd been warned of—and stories about things that had never happened seemed a more honest approximation of truth.

Years later in grad school, when other white women talked about imposter syndrome, I was unsympathetic. I'd never suffered any doubts about my analytic or communicative abilities, my absolute belonging in the hermeneutics of useless conclusions. And anyway, I knew what it felt like to be a real imposter, standing in chapel, singing behind Miriam as she dipped boisterously into the tenor line.

When the cone finally came off my head that day, when my joy came to an end, it was not I who removed the tall, triangular covering, but my computer teacher, Melissa. And even though the first thing I saw when the orange glow lifted from my eyes was her frown, she raised it gently and never said a word.

The blessed assurance of those days had already begun to trickle away, and as time slipped along beside it, my surety washed by in waves. Still, when these memories rise up in me now, carrying with them a crushing love for those people and that place, my faith in them refuses to be shaken. Perhaps I sensed, even then, despite my hopeful longing for the future, that such happiness would not so easily be found again, which is why on my last day, I reached for a hymnal and then secreted the book out of the building, the only object I have ever stolen. When I open it and sit at the piano, the blue binding cracks. I press the keys slowly, slowly, straining to hear what was, what might have been.

ACKNOWLEDGEMENTS

If you have just read this book, you may recall that I've spent a lot of time editing other authors' acknowledgements. You might pardon me, then, for struggling to do this unironically.

A few of the essays gathered here first appeared in earlier forms in the following publications: "Vegetable Psychology, Lovesick Astrology" in *Harpur Palate*, "Moving" in *Saranac Review*, "The Trouble with Loving Poets" in *Hippocampus*, and "Hung Up" in *The Missouri Review* online. I thank the editors and staff of these journals.

Many *more* of these essays were rejected from the following publications: *DIAGRAM, River Teeth, The Pinch, Word Riot, Salon, Conjunctions, Fourth Genre, The Butter, Indiana Review, Sweet Lit, swamp pink, The Cincinnati Review, Michigan Quarterly Review, Alaska Quarterly Review, A Public Space, West Branch, The Gettysburg Review* (RIP), *AGNI, Colorado Review, Tin House, Ploughshares, Black Warrior Review, Bat City Review, Cream City Review, Creative Nonfiction, Ninth Letter, Brevity, The Sun, Hayden's Ferry Review, Gulf Coast, Iron Horse Literary Review, The Rumpus, Subtropics, Orion, The Kenyon Review, The American Scholar*, and, of course, *The New York Times*.

Some of these essays have been in process for twenty years—not because they were rejected by lots of publications but because that's how long it took me to finish this book. It was not until I bought a house and stayed in one place for more than two years that I had the kind of stability I needed to do that, and for providing that stability, I sincerely thank the NeighborWorks program in Lincoln, Nebraska (and, for paying me so little that I qualified for the housing assistance that begot some of the happiest and most productive years of my life, credit goes to UNP).

My sincere gratitude goes to Chloé Cooper Jones for selecting an earlier version of what became this book as the runner-up for AWP's Sue William Silverman Prize. Such a vote of confidence from a writer I so deeply admire was incredibly validating, and it made all the difference in finding a great home for this book. Thank you.

I have many people to thank at Ohio State, chief among them Michelle and Andrew, Doug and Scott, and Allison, Ava, and Preston. My thanks go especially to Nina and Megan, for years of great advice and even better company. Thanks, too, to my OSU colleagues at the press, where I am lucky to work.

Thank you, always, to my family, as well as to the many other people in this book who shaped it. I hope that where I've inevitably failed, I've at least done so in interesting or entertaining ways.

ABOUT THE AUTHOR

Elizabeth Zaleski grew up in rural northeast Ohio. After living and traveling all over the country, she now lives in slightly less rural northeast Ohio, outside Akron. She works as an editor and is the curator of GreatFartsofLiterature.com. Her essays have appeared in journals such as *Hippocampus, The Normal School,* and *The Missouri Review.*

Belt Publishing

beltpublishing.com